D1587218

L.M.S. LOCOMOTIVE IN PERSIA TAKING SUPPLIES TO RUSSIA

THE LMS AT WAR

By

GEORGE C. NASH

(G. C. N. of *Punch*)

Published by

THE LONDON MIDLAND AND SCOTTISH RAILWAY

EUSTON

C 6188 270-4

First published 1946

HERTFORDSHIRE
COUNTY LIBRARY

385.094

2082080

MADE AND PRINTED IN GREAT BRITAIN
BY JARROLD AND SONS, LTD., EMPIRE PRESS, NORWICH

CONTENTS

LIST OF ILLUSTRATIONS

The illustrations in colour are from originals executed for the Company by Norman Wilkinson, O.B.E., P.R.I.

CHAPTER ONE

L.M.S.

JOHN BULL uses initials extensively. They save him a lot of trouble. He has his R.A.F., his W.R.N.S., his B.Sc., and his G.H.Q.—he even has his l.b.w. They slip off his tongue without any difficulty and sometimes he forgets exactly what they stand for. When the London Midland and Scottish Railway Company came into being little more than twenty years ago, he found it something of a mouthful. London Midland and Scottish—London *and* Midland *and* Scottish or just plain London Midland Scottish, he was never quite sure which it was. While north of the Border, and possibly on patriotic grounds, there was a tendency to move "Scottish" a bit more to the forefront and call it London Scottish and Midland. Often, too, he found it difficult to remember if the Company was "Limited."

But in the end John Bull got over all his difficulties and referred to this vast undertaking as the L.M.S., and white on black, gold on crimson and in many other colours these three familiar letters spread through the land and became a household affair.

The chapters which follow will give an account of the L.M.S. at war, but before the story is unfolded it is necessary to refer very briefly to the Company's pre-war history and activities. Given such a background a better conception will be obtained of what the railway did during the years that lay ahead of that fateful day in September, 1939, when Adolf Hitler attacked Poland and began the Second World War.

Before and during the First World War of 1914–18, Great Britain possessed some 120 companies, each of which was separately constituted. But with the passing of the Railways Act of 1921 these companies were amalgamated into the four great organizations we know to-day—the L.M.S., the L.N.E.R., the G.W.R. and the Southern. And the biggest of that Big Four was the L.M.S. To its share fell the old London and North Western, the Midland, the Caledonian, the Furness, the Glasgow and South Western, the Lancashire and Yorkshire, the North Staffordshire and the Highland, together with 27 subsidiary companies. Ramifications which reached from Goole on the East Coast of England to Donegal Bay on the West Coast of Ireland and from Bournemouth on the English Channel to Thurso in the far north of Scotland; the whole layout covering nearly 40 per cent of the total route mileage of the railways of England, Scotland and Wales.

It was only natural therefore that when the amalgamation under the Railways Act took effect on January 1st, 1923, many years of arduous work lay ahead. Those diverse companies had to be welded into a unified whole, equipment and procedure standardized, dead wood removed, rationalization and modernization adopted. This and much more was duly carried out, so that by the summer of 1939, and indeed for some years before that date, everything was working at a very high state of efficiency.

The principal function of a railway company is the movement of passengers and goods, and the L.M.S. had 19,000 track miles and a staff of some 250,000 persons to do it with. And on those track miles and with that staff, aided by 7,500 engines and 303,000 separate pieces of rolling stock, it was carrying in 1939 some 434,000,000 passengers, representing

7,500,000,000 miles of travel, and 125,000,000 tons of freight, representing 6,750,000,000 ton-miles.

But that is not the full measure of what the peacetime L.M.S. stood for. It owned 25 docks, harbours and piers, hundreds of acres of engineering workshops, 66 steamships, 4,000 motors and 3,000 trailers, 8,000 horses, 28 hotels, 25,000 dwelling houses, aeroplanes, and 535 miles of canals. In addition they were caterers, warehousemen, launderers, and household removal agents on an extensive scale; its more peculiar activities running from pig farming to supplying gas to a town of 50,000 inhabitants.

Between 1923 and 1938 it is interesting to see how the L.M.S. fulfilled its various obligations to the British public under the Railways Act of 1921. During that time millions of pounds were spent on rolling stock and on the permanent way. New locomotives, carriages, wagons and steamships were constructed. Stations, goods depots, hotels, workshops, docks and warehouses were built or modernized. Tracks were doubled and even quadrupled, while schemes of electrification were put in hand and completed. Indeed the pre-war replacement cost of the Company's property was conservatively estimated to exceed £750,000,000.

Comfort, speed, safety, efficiency and punctuality became the railwayman's gods. Standards in travel comfort were set high. Third-class sleepers were introduced. Restaurant cars were increased in number. Cheap fares were popularized. So far as freight was concerned new types of carrying vehicles were designed to cater for all kinds of traffic, such as door-to-door containers, road-rail tanks, refrigerators, shock-absorbing wagons. Anything from milk to elephants and from coal to cucumbers, the L.M.S. delivered the goods.

Fast locomotives of new design like the "Coronation" swung north up the backbone of England at over a mile a minute (there were 67 daily trains scheduled to run more than 60 miles per hour in 1938). Development was always going on. New devices, new methods —colour light signalling, automatic train control, solid fuel cooking for restaurant cars, accelerated shunting methods, (layout, mechanical braking, and lighting). The railway would take John Bull, his wife, child and dog for a holiday, house, feed and amuse them when they got them there, and bring them back again. Choice of accommodation ran from a railway caravan on the banks of a salmon river in the Highlands, by way of an up-to-date holiday camp, to a suite of rooms in a first-class hotel in any one of a dozen important cities up and down the land.

With all this and much more it will be seen that when the Government took control of the railways on September 1st, 1939, the L.M.S.—the greatest of all privately owned railway companies—passed, for the duration of the war, into the national service of the country at the highest degree of maintenance and operating efficiency it had ever attained.

CHAPTER TWO

FROM PEACE TO WAR

THE most successful nation in war is the nation with the most efficient transport. Hannibal, with his desert-bred horses, pack animals and elephants realized this when in 218 B.C. he made his rapid thrust through Spain and Gaul to cross the Alps into the heart of Italy. Jenghiz Khan realized it well over a thousand years later when he swept from the China Seas to the Dnieper. Cromwell, Marlborough, Napoleon, Foch, and all in increasing degree, knew the value of good transport and its supreme importance in battle. How much more then would transport matter in the war that was coming, and where the heavier weapons and fire-power of 600 men were reckoned to equal that of 20,000 men in 1918.

Railways, it was obvious, would be well to the fore in attack or defence. Railways fighting with their tracks and their engines. That Great Britain had the most concentrated and intricate railway system in the world was a fact of the greatest strategic importance.

In international politics the late 1930's were uneasy years for the railways, and in 1937 war was regarded as more than a possibility. After that date it was a probability, and when the Czechoslovakian crisis came in March, 1939, an easy-money bet. Germany stank of gunpowder from end to end and the fuse was burning.

Some years before 1939 mild discussions took place and some plans were even ready for a switch over to war, but after Munich the pace was speeded up and preparations were of a different character. Outwardly business was carried on as usual, but behind closed doors there were secret meetings and discussions, and in April, 1939, instructions were published that in an emergency the Minister of Transport would be responsible for the provision, allotment and co-ordination of internal transport services, and the railways brought under his control—an arrangement which did not in any way mean that the L.M.S. would lose its identity or *esprit de corps*.

The main lines of war policy as between the Government and the railways were then worked out by a small Railway Executive Committee whose principal function was to act as adviser to, and the agent of, the Minister of War Transport. The instructions of this committee covering the movement of men and war materials, and the distribution of essential supplies, being so planned that they could be executed by each of the railway companies through their existing organizations—officers and staff remaining responsible to their own managements and boards as in peacetime.

Throughout the period of hostilities, therefore, the task of the Company was two-fold. Firstly to see that the integrity and smooth working of the Company were preserved and its affairs so directed that it could carry out efficiently and economically the instructions of the Railway Executive Committee in terms of Government policy. Secondly, to continue to discharge those of its own innumerable day-to-day functions in which the Government had no real or direct interest.

The setting up of this committee was followed by active planning between Government departments, the services and the main-line railway companies. There were Regional

Transport Committees and Port Emergency Committees, Railway Traffic Officers, Railway Liaison Officers, and a host of others. Responsibilities extended from schemes for the execution of major troop movements to the conveyance of a single naval gun. And always with the prime objective: that the most effective and economical use could be made of every locomotive, carriage and wagon.

A complete revision of the conditions under which the railways would operate in war was then undertaken. The wheels had to be kept moving and used to the best purpose. The quick movement of men, raw materials and munitions was all important, while supplies necessary to maintain the life of the nation as a whole had to be distributed to every corner of the land. Detailed work in the compilation of schemes and schedules was carried out, and often there were drastic revisions in the light of some change of Government policy. But whatever was done and planned it became obvious that the L.M.S., in view of its size and geographical spread, would have to bear the heaviest railway burden of all.

There was much to engage the higher executive's attention, for each of the big national issues extensively affected the Company's internal affairs. The evacuation of the civilian population from the vulnerable areas, the transfer of commodities away from the ports— the Port of London especially—and the problems arising from possible invasion.

The fighting services, it was clearly recognized, would make extensive calls including mobilization and the despatch of an expeditionary force overseas. Transportation, sidings and tracks would be required for the new factories that were springing up all over the country. There were, too, the vast complications which would have to be faced, if and when it became a strategic necessity to divert rail traffic away from the east side of the land to the west, or from the west to the east. A glance at the map of the L.M.S. system will show how much additional work this alone would throw on the railway, and for either contingency plans were required in advance. The curtailment of the ordinary civilian and holiday traffic was another big problem for which nearly every one of the 1,138 pages of the 1939 "Bradshaw" would have to be overhauled and put on a war footing.

In all these matters the L.M.S. operating department, with a pre-war strength greatly exceeding the whole personnel of the peacetime Royal Navy, began to peer into a future dark with uncertainties.

Other departments had their problems too. The huge workshops in the Midlands and the North, in addition to tackling urgent orders for anything from new locomotives to handbarrows, were busy with the fitting of ambulance trains for the services and for the civilian population. They undertook as early as 1937 the design of a medium tank, and later the manufacture of aeroplane wings and other parts, together with the repair of damaged aircraft and the reforming of cartridge cases—jobs which at the peak period actually absorbed 32 per cent of the labour in their workshops.

Everywhere there was much guesswork. The railway would be bombed. That was a certainty—but how and where? Would such bombing be concentrated or dispersed over a wide area? Would the east or the west get the brunt of the attack, bridges or moving trains, warehouses or the large marshalling yards? The horrors of poison gas, at this time, had to be reckoned as probable.

Eventually plans were evolved on the lines that bombing would come by day and night, that there would be interim attacks on the large industrial centres, that the key positions on the railways would be singled out for special attention and that rail communications would be cut wherever possible. Large numbers of the staff, it was assumed, would not be able to reach their jobs for long periods, and that repair work would have to be proceeded with under conditions of restricted lighting and perhaps in the presence of poison gas.

In the light of all this, further schemes had to be prepared against air raids and for the dissemination of air raid warnings. A vast construction and building programme for shelters was embarked on; and the windows of the signal boxes were covered with cellophane and hessian. Even old engine boiler barrels were earmarked as possible auxiliary shelters and six miles of trenches dug, while rescue parties and decontamination squads were formed and trained wherever it was considered necessary. The issue of wartime instructions to the Company's 250,000 employees was a job in itself.

One of the biggest headaches of all was the blackout—and throughout the story which follows, this was probably the railwayman's greatest burden of all. It tried his temper to the uttermost, and the train hours lost due to speed retardation were impossible to compute. With every electric globe, lamp, torch and lantern to be seen to, "light" comedy during this particular change-over was provided by a local officer who wrote asking for the removal of a shade which had been fixed to a lamp as a blackout restriction in the 1914–18 war! A request which though reasonable in itself was felt to be singularly ill-timed.

And so it went on. Docks and permanent way, signals and telegraphs, hotels, refreshment rooms, air services, stores, canals—all had their worries, and extensive and peculiar they often were.

Take communications. Without communication a railway is like a human being without a brain. Fortunately in pre-war days the Company had a first-class and very comprehensive system both for the conduct of ordinary business and for traffic control purposes. This, however, had to be added to extensively—emergency control offices, telephone exchanges, telegraph offices, transportable carrier systems, wireless telegraphy, wireless telephones, and by the laying in of immense stores.

If the normal channels were cut, a second and often a third and a fourth alternative was made ready, and in one way or another, thousands of miles of telephone line were erected by the Signal and Telegraph Engineer's department, who in the course of time also erected 100 new signal boxes (5,400 additional levers and 2,800 new signals).

Over and above all this hung the problem of shortage of staff. The call-up of trained men to the forces, and the drain of others to the better-paid jobs in the munition factories had to be faced, and good railwaymen are not made in a day.

At first sight it might not appear to be a very difficult undertaking to convert an organization like the L.M.S. from peace to war. In peacetime it carries human beings and freight, in war it is the same. But apart from what has already been described there were other broad facts which had to be faced, and in particular—that where the railway in peacetime worked for seven days a week with a 24-hour day, factories, generally speaking, were only working five and a half days a week on say an eight-hour shift, and in war those factories, or many of them, would be keyed up to 24 hours a day for seven days a week. Such a difference, even allowing for the fact that some non-essential factories might be closing down, gave the railway and especially the operating department much anxiety and deep thought.

Industrial concerns usually complete long-range programmes of their requirements in men and especially in material and machines. The L.M.S. is no exception. In peacetime, traffic requirements were anticipated to a degree of precision. Passengers and goods ran in well-defined flows. Variations in volume were forecast season by season. But preparation for the construction of say locomotives and wagons and for the recruitment and training of men, such as engine drivers, must be made in advance.

It was obvious therefore that train crews, locomotives and rolling stock would be pressed as never before in the history of the Company. For in spite of the fact that the Company possessed a sufficient margin of reserves for peak demands like the summer holiday traffic and the transport of winter coal, being a private company and run by private enterprise and with no Government subsidy—indeed the L.M.S. often helped the Government, especially with unemployment relief schemes—it would have been guilty if it had carried surplus assets greater than were justified by the tasks it was likely to be required to perform.

It had, too, always been assumed that the railways had unlimited resources to move any class of goods in any quantity to any destination at a moment's notice, but it was a long time before the large production departments of the Ministry of Supply, the Ministry of Aircraft Production and the Admiralty realized that although this might be all very well in peacetime, conditions imposed by war revolutionized the entire set-up.

There were many initial difficulties by reason of the fact that each of these departments often worked independently and often in direct conflict so that from a railway point of view there was much waste of time and power. Slowly, however, some sort of real co-ordination was attained, though frequently forecasts of requirements by the fighting services and Government departments were so indefinite in regard to time and place as to be of little assistance.

So those tense summer days of 1939 passed slowly on. The newspaper headlines tell their own story. "Government Decide to Recall Parliament;" "Russo-German Treaty Signed;" "Hitler Presides over German War Council;" "Britain Delivers Final Warning to Berlin" . . .

When war was inevitable in the last week of August, the preliminary stages of the change-over were set in motion. Naval mobilization had been in progress for some time. Now general mobilization was ordered and a start made with the despatch of our expeditionary force overseas. Holiday-makers returned home. Lighting restrictions were enforced. Evacuation started.

On September 1st the Government assumed control of the railways and the Railway Executive Committee took over. To the general public the change was particularly pronounced, for where the railways had for years encouraged travel it was now discouraged. But when the storm broke at 11 a.m. on September 3rd the L.M.S. was ready. The "phoney war" and the "sitzkrieg" had begun.

CHAPTER THREE

EVACUATION

A RAILWAY STATION sees life from a peculiar angle—beginnings and ends, arrivals and departures, happy home-comings and sad good-byes. The vast exodus of children which took place from many of the largest cities of Great Britain in the first four days of September, 1939, was unique among such scenes.

Known as the Evacuation, it was probably the greatest controlled mass movement of human beings within so short a time that the world had ever seen. A page in the nation's history, and at the same time a page in the intimate diary of millions of British homes up and down the land.

Railway plans for the Evacuation were first made in the autumn of 1938, and overhauled in July, 1939. They were drawn up so that they could be quickly set in motion, and in point of fact less than 24 hours sufficed. The decision was taken on August 31st, and next morning tens of thousands of children were being shepherded from school assembly points to the main-line and suburban railway stations.

The L.M.S. handled much of this traffic. It came in a steady flow to 15 of the Company's stations, 1,450 special trains were run, and on the evening of the fourth day the total number of passengers dealt with was returned as approximately half a million. And allw ithout a single casualty, and all interwoven with the extensive ordinary summer services then still running. Even the Company's London electric service was hard at it (one train every eight minutes) taking passengers out of the city to where steam trains waited to move them farther afield.

The children, some accompanied by their mothers, but generally by school officials, ranged from 3 to 13 years of age. Each child carried a gas mask, food, a change of clothing and wore three labels. As they entered the railway stations they marched with a good step, but many of their little faces were hard set trying to be brave. Amongst them there were Jewish children from Berlin, and one child who had arrived from Danzig only a few hours previously.

During those four days the railway staff on duty in the stations acted as guide, philosopher and friend to many bewildered little people. It was a job different from routine. The children were leaving their *homes*, and in spite of many outwardly cheery faces it was a picture pathetically sad. As train after train pulled out to the safe areas some of the staff must have looked wistfully after them, perhaps especially remembering a little girl of ten, who in parting from her mother had said: "Will I ever see you again, Mummy, here or anywhere else?"

No one knew. The war machine of the Hun had been set in motion and perhaps with the advent of the next batch of children that same railway station on which they were standing might be a shambles of twisted girders and broken bodies. The war of nerves was still no idle phrase.

Some trains ran to destinations 200 miles away. They made various halts en route and bachelor stationmasters in country towns were soon facing the most embarrassing domestic situations, but—to give them their due—with a lack of bashfulness that must have surprised even themselves.

At the many points of final detrainment, station staffs were also busy. Much however, had been done beforehand to make things as easy as possible for everyone. The railways had even carried food to storage places in many reception areas, so that rations could be supplied to the travellers before they went to their new billets.

But that was only part of the railway's work during those busy days. Great Britain at that time was like a huge ants' nest that had been disturbed by some outside force, and in the months and years that lay ahead there were further extensive stirrings of the community. In addition to the children, and even before the war, many of the public were busy evacuating themselves. Hospitals, Government departments and big business firms were also early astir. The Bank of England staff had gone, requiring two special trains to shift its offices, records and equipment.

One of the biggest and speediest moves was accomplished by the L.M.S. itself when it transferred its headquarters out of London. Following Italy's invasion of Albania in the Easter week-end of 1939 the Company took over a large vacant country house in Hertford-shire. This was made ready as offices, and a number of huts built in the surrounding park. On Friday, September 1st, it was decided to move in, and the transfer was completed before war was declared on Sunday at 11 a.m. In a few hours, therefore, Euston had temporarily ceased to be the headquarters of the Company, and on Monday, September 4th, 3,000 of the staff were at work in their new establishment. In miniature it was like trans-ferring the Government of a country from its capital to a provincial town.

And so it went on. Boarding schools left the south of England for Scotland, Americans were conveyed to Eire en route for home. Dutch, Belgian and French women and thousands of children arrived from the Continent seeking sanctuary.

There was mobilization, there was Dunkirk (to be referred to later), and there was the arrival on the South Coast of many homeless Channel Islanders which required the running of 29 trains to L.M.S. destinations.

From the influx of refugees from Gibraltar to the departure of children to the Dominions and the U.S.A., the Company did its bit. It even removed the Italian Embassy staff and a large number of Italians to the docks at Glasgow when Mussolini declared war on a tottering France.

Followed the extensive evacuation of civilians when London was first bombed—and later as the enemy turned his attention to the systematic destruction of the provincial centres—more large movements, including schoolchildren and whole families, were carried by the railways to outlying areas.

The L.M.S. at this time was specially busy in Birmingham, Coventry, Liverpool, Birkenhead, Manchester and Salford, but in April, 1941, it was Glasgow, when 27 special trains were required for the evacuation of registered schoolchildren. The next month, Liverpool, under sustained night attacks by the Luftwaffe, had a different problem, and the Company took entire households out of the city in controlled trains which ran every evening from 7.30 p.m. at fifteen-minute intervals. Those trains, moreover, never stopped until all the passengers had been safely got away, and the next morning they were busy again returning the working members to their jobs.

Evacuation, however, was both organized and unorganized, and sometimes it worked in reverse when many people, especially before Christmas, 1939, returned to their homes in the cities. But it did not stop at passengers. Many different types of freight were also moved. In September, 1939, for instance, large quantities of art treasures and irreplaceable historic specimens were packed up and taken from the National Gallery, the British Museum, the Tate Gallery and Westminster Abbey. The precious nature of these consignments involved a great deal of specialized planning, and there was much earnest discussion over strange-looking packages, between officials of the institutions concerned and the loading experts of the railway's operating department.

Then too, there was the "evacuation" of food. The transfer of meat and butter away from the Port of London. Between August 31st and September 4th, 1939—32 special trains were run by the L.M.S.—12 of them to G.W. destinations, and a few days later the Company sent a further 7 specials to convey 1,600 tons of tea to the north.

All of the movements described in this chapter, of passengers or freight, required forethought and planning. They were conferences in the L.M.S. offices and elsewhere both before and after the outbreak of war. Many of the plans made in minute detail (against enemy invasion, etc.) were never used, and many others had to be changed at a moment's notice in the light of altered conditions.

So much then for the railway's part in evacuation. But what might have been? On September 11th, 1939, a train of evacuees left Warsaw for Lwow. During the journey passengers had to take cover from German bombers on 72 occasions. There were many casualties.

CHAPTER FOUR

AIR RAID PRECAUTIONS

WAR conditions affected the railwayman's work extensively. They faced him wherever he went, and like the farmer, the fisherman, the shopkeeper or the office worker, he could rarely get the subject out of his head. His life was a mass of regulations, restrictions and warning notices. He dreamed trains, thought of trains, ate in them and slept beside them. The personnel and munitions of war streamed in a never-ending flow through his hands. Mortar shells, W.A.A.F.s, aeroplane engines, admirals, tanks, prisoners of war, the flow was constant and unceasing night and day. But it was A.R.P. that really made him sore, and it was no stirrup pump and Anderson shelter affair that fell to his lot.

In order therefore, to see what A.R.P. meant both to the higher executives of the L.M.S. and to the working railwayman himself, the more important features will be now reviewed, so that a better idea may be obtained of the conditions under which the Company came eventually to fight the Battle of the Railways.

Take first of all the formidable tasks which confronted the higher executives. These can be grouped under two main headings: (*a*) to keep traffic moving even during the progress of an air raid; and (*b*) the protection of their enormous staff.

These points engaged their attention from the time of the Austrian Anschluss in 1938, and thereafter, in varying degrees, throughout the war. The working of the trains, both passenger and freight, was a problem. How were moving trains to be warned? What was to happen to the passengers? How fast could trains travel? And each problem had to be examined from two angles, the night and the day, and always the maximum amount of traffic had to be worked.

The dissemination of air raid warnings to the companies' stations, yards and depots was a vast job, and the problems themselves always difficult. There were meetings with the Home Office and the General Post Office, and here again two features had to receive first care—the speedy reception and dissemination of warnings and the limitation of the areas warned to the smallest, so as not to retard the movement of transport unnecessarily. All these plans were subject to constant revision and alteration, and many improvements originally suggested by the Company were accepted by the Government for adoption by railways as a whole.

The planning for the protection of the staff greyed many an officer's head. Personnel who had to remain at their posts during air raids had to have good protection, and naturally, control staffs, traffic staffs at marshalling yards, motive power staffs at engine sheds, signalmen, telephone and telegraph operators must have prior attention.

The Divisional and District Control Offices, for instance—the operating nerve centres of the railways—had to be provided with alternative protective office accommodation, in which the staff could carry on their work whatever the conditions outside. Two types of emergency control offices were designed—some of fortress-like dimensions, with roofs 10 feet thick, others in the less vulnerable areas, capable of withstanding blast and splinters.

Signalboxes were the subject of innumerable experiments before final plans were

L.M.S. STEAMERS *PRINCESS MAUD* AND *DUCHESS OF YORK* EVACUATING TROOPS FROM ST. VALÉRY UNDER SHELL-FIRE

evolved, which included steel shelters and plates, bricking up, sandbagging and the provision of concrete roofs. The large glass windows in the majority of signalboxes were extremely difficult to protect, and as has already been told these were covered with cellophane or hessian. The results however, were effective, as this report from a stationmaster will show:

On December 23rd, 1940, I was on duty at Victoria West Junction signalbox. At about 11.50 p.m. I was on the telephone when suddenly the signalman shouted. I saw a blue flash, followed by a terrific explosion. Then the window facing the station blew in on me and wrapped itself around my head. Thanks to the cellophane covering it saved my face and head from serious injury. I was flung to the floor and, recovering very quickly, I went to the signalman to see if he was all right. He was rather shocked, like myself. We then set about clearing the debris from the cabin.

Not only had marshalling yards, motive power depots, workshops, goods and passenger stations their own particular and peculiar problems, but hotels, steamers, aeroplanes, docks, all had to be thought of.

The camouflage of buildings and bulk materials such as stocks of timber, was also undertaken, and a large collection of stores for emergency repairs got together and distributed in selected spots about the country. These stores ran to thousands of separate items, from bridges and entire signalboxes (in sections), down to minute screws for delicate wireless apparatus.

Another responsibility of the Executive was the training of the staff in general A.R.P. work, fire fighting, first aid, gas decontamination, together with emergency repair gangs for many different types of job, including the clearance of wreckage.

It was, of course, quite impossible for shelter accommodation to be provided for the passenger, but where protection was not available in the shape of subways, notices were posted in the stations indicating the location of the nearest public shelter. The passenger, generally speaking, was, however, essentially philosophical during an air raid, and especially if he was in a moving train. Perhaps he consoled himself with the fact that it is always more difficult to hit a flying bird, or perhaps it was due to the A.R.P. notice which first appeared in railway compartments a few days before war broke out:

. . . . "Do not attempt to leave the train if it stops away from a station, unless requested by the guard to do so".

The fact that a railway guard could still "request" was reassuring. Things might be worse. In Germany they would have been "ordered."

.   .   .   .   .

The working railwayman had many responsibilities in A.R.P., but it was the blackout that gave him the most trouble. In peacetime, modern railway practice demands efficient lighting. Artificial daylight was the standard aimed at, and to this end, pre-war, the L.M.S. spent large sums of money. When precautions against air attack were first mooted, lighting came prominently to the fore, the Government's ideal being a complete blackout of the entire country.

Naturally this would lead to many serious repercussions at every external centre on the railway system, and many internal—for outside work at night would be more or less brought to a standstill.

The question, therefore, was first referred to a Lighting Committee, consisting of representatives of the Ministry of Transport, the Home Office, the Air Ministry and the railway companies, and several tests carried out to ascertain the minimum amount of light which would be required.

B

Agreement was eventually reached on the lines that if the essential railway services were to be operated with reasonable safety and reasonable speed, a complete blackout was not generally practicable.

The upshot of all this was that every railway point, large and small, was classified for lighting restrictions into three main groups. The most important places—and relatively they were not many—having "exempted" lighting (extinguished on receipt of an air raid warning). Others, "fully restricted" lighting (unextinguished on an air raid warning or during an air raid, and sarcastically known as "Gloomy Glim," and frequently something much worse!). The remainder, complete blackout.

Vast preparations were finally made for these changes, which also covered train lighting, firebox glow, dimming signal lights and the blacking out of glass on station roofs. Restricted lighting on trains alone required the replacement of no fewer than 150,000 electric bulbs.

Everyone was affected by the blackout. The engine driver lost his comforting landmarks up and down the line—the cathedral, the gasworks, the familiar glow from the local foundry. He had difficulties in stopping his train at the right place in dimmed-out stations. His footplate was stifling hot due to the anti-glare sheets which enclosed his cab, so as to prevent glow from the firebox being visible to raiders, and he had immense difficulties in learning a new line.

The shunter in the large marshalling yard, where 2,000 trucks were sometimes dealt with in a single night, referred to the blackout with venom. During air raid warnings, when his lights were shut off entirely he had to rely on handlamps. Wagon after wagon moving up out of the inky darkness, and visible at only a yard or two, had to be controlled and kept moving. The work was arduous and dangerous, and called for intense concentration. Ice on the sidetracks made things worse, the addition of fog worse still. The job was often a nightmare.

But all through the service it was the same. Signalmen could rarely get visible confirmation of the speed or the length of each train that entered and left their particular section. In motive power depots the problems concerned the screening of frost fires, the glow of ashes, minor repairs and cleaning. Drivers of electric trains had to exercise particular care against "arcing" on the lines, having to coast over all points, crossings, and gaps (so as to reduce flash to a minimum) and in the vast workshops and goods depots, work, in daylight, often went on under the disability of blacked-out roof lights.

From the hotel "Boots" to the air pilot, and from the ticket collector to the master of one of the Company's Irish cross-channel vessels, literally feeling his way into and out of harbour—each had his own dilemmas and perplexities.

And always there was the added anxiety that belongs to all wartime jobs. This, in the more responsible railway posts, meant the safe carrying of the precious burden of human lives, the vital munitions and materials of the services and the foodstuffs of the nation.

Granted that conditions were alleviated in small particulars as the war progressed, but theirs was the responsibility, night in, night out, from one end of the country to the other, on land, on sea, and in the air. It is to their everlasting credit that accidents were so few and far between.

And so it was that from September 1st, 1939, when the Minister of Transport directed that the new system of lighting be adopted, the railways started to face up to what the Operating Manager of the L.M.S. described as the greatest and most widespread single disability which they had ever had to meet. It was hell!

CHAPTER FIVE

WORK FOR THE SERVICES—1939-1945

IN war, the movement of troops by rail, together with their equipment and armour, is a tricky business with peculiar and inherent characteristics. It can be called for at a moment's notice on a priority basis. It has no regular ebb and flow. It is uncertain in quantity. Furthermore, it involves an unbelievable amount of preparatory work, in that it has to be woven into the already complicated pattern of civilian train timings.

And no one who has not had the privilege of watching the work that went on behind the scenes at the height of the colossal movements of troops and munitions, at busy centres like Crewe, can have any idea of what was accomplished by the staff.

Rail transport for the services varied from the conveyance of small parties by ordinary passenger train to large concentrations requiring 300 specials, and from single wagons carrying a solitary piece of equipment to as many as 50 trains loaded with tanks and Bren-gun carriers.

Sometimes these trains had to run from one side of the country to the other, and often, especially where the L.M.S. was concerned, from camps in the south of England to training grounds on little single-track lines in the bleak and sparsely populated districts of the far north, where stations were frequently ill-equipped to handle such traffic.

In the 1914–18 war the majority of our troops were fighting abroad, and Britain only held reserves and men under training. But in this war, after the collapse of France—British, Dominion, Colonial, American and other Allied forces, trained and under training, were assembled in all parts of the land. There was no really big outlet for them overseas until equipment had been made good and shipping was available. Moreover, the threat of invasion demanded their detention until the outlook grew less dark.

As the strength and size of the Allied war machine developed and expanded, so service traffic on the railways increased, and as each month went by, it reached bigger and bigger proportions until eventually it became phenomenal. Indeed the strain at one time nearly broke the camel's back—and it was some camel!

In the light of all this it is astonishing that in peacetime, criticism had actually been levelled at the railways on the basis that they would be so vulnerable to enemy attack during a war that immediate provision should be made for the expansion of other forms of transport. Indeed, a Northern Ireland Parliamentary Committee had actually stated that the railways in that country were not essential for troop movements in time of war! In the following chapters it will be seen how supremely essential the railways actually were to the nation in these, the most hazardous years of its history.

PERSONNEL

To begin at the beginning. Mobilization. Naval mobilization had been going on gradually during the summer of 1939, and was accomplished with little more than the ordinary passenger service. But mobilization of the Army and Air Force was a different proposition.

It commenced on Saturday, September 2nd—when the evacuation of the children was at its peak—and was spread over 24 days, involving the running of 164 special trains* by the L.M.S. alone.

Over and above these extensive movements two expeditionary forces were proceeding to the Continent. Both were the particular care of the Company. The first, prior to the outbreak of war, was safely carried for embarkation to Glasgow. The second, to the same port, took place between September 7th and October 7th.

For the next few months the Company was mainly concerned with the conveyance of men called to the forces, with the posting of Army and Air Force personnel to units after training was completed, and with work in connection with the "phoney" war in France.

Next month saw the despatch of our Expeditionary Force to Norway, with 202 trains running mainly to Glasgow and Leith, and including a rush transportation of three trainloads of French troops from one end of the country to the other.

Came Dunkirk—summed up in the words of the operating department as follows:

> This evacuation gave the railways the opportunity of performing what was, without doubt, a remarkable feat in the transport world. Personnel of the Allied armies withdrawn from Northern France were disembarked at almost every available pier or dock along the south-east coast, and loaded in waiting trains which were sent to intermediate regulatory points where military officers and railway officials were in attendance to decide the ultimate destination of each train. As the number of troops to be conveyed, and the rate of their arrival on shore could not be gauged, the whole of this movement, known as "Operation Dynamo," which was undertaken at extremely short notice, was organized and executed as circumstances dictated. All trains were controlled by telephone, as it was impossible, in view of the circumstances, to schedule timings. A common pool of railway coaching stock was created, to which the L.M.S. contributed 44 trains out of a total of 186 concentrated for the purpose.
>
> The complete movement was accomplished efficiently, and the Secretary of State for War published a statement in the Press which recorded his appreciation of the satisfactory arrangements made by the railway companies. The bulk of the work devolved upon the Southern Railway, but the L.M.S. collaborated to the fullest extent required. A total of 319,116 troops in 620 trains were worked away from the disembarkation points to reception areas in all parts of the country, the whole of the movement being performed in 16 days."

It was indeed a remarkable feat, everyone was on the job, and drivers, guards and firemen often worked 18 hours at a stretch.

A short lull and the railways were again in the thick of things with more emergency calls. Twelve days after Dunkirk, Allied personnel from the more westerly and south-westerly coasts of France arrived at ports in the south and west of England. Wear yand worn, they came, with wisecrack and grim jest, and out of 200 trains required to move them inland, the L.M.S. worked 123, which included three specials for French munition workers.

The speed and withdrawal of our troops left a disorganized army spread over the face of the country, and the railways were immediately faced with the problem of providing transport to take troops to military depots for reorganization and re-equipment. Leave followed almost at once for nearly everyone, and there was a further ebb and flow. The nation had had a bad fall. She was stunned and her recovery, it was obvious, would take some time.

· · · · ·

So began the long build-up to D-Day—the years of blood and toil, of tears and sweat.

*An average troop train carries 500 passengers.

To begin with there were many extensive internal movements. Large forces were sent to Northern Ireland to strengthen the garrison there. L.M.S. steamers and trains took a big part in this, and all civilian passenger sailings on the former were cancelled. There were also redistributional changes when the railways were often called upon to carry whole army divisions from one area to another.

At this time, too, the Navy made occasional calls for transport, and the Air Force was busy fitting up its new aerodromes as and when they became ready for use and occupation.

Troops for active service, garrison duties or training went to the Mediterranean, India and the Far East and to Iceland, South Africa, Canada and the U.S.A. The largest repositioning of troops in Great Britain took place in February and March, 1941, when huge bodies of men were moved to strategic areas for the protection of the country against enemy invasion, and although the majority of them travelled by road, the L.M.S. had a big share of the rail traffic.

In May, 1942, a complicated shift was made from remote parts of Scotland to the Isle of Wight. It included the transport of troops, Bren-gun carriers, bridging materials, guns, tractors and an unusual amount of baggage. Three weeks later they all had to be returned to their original starting points.

But thousands of moves were made here, there and everywhere, and all required constant liaison, and plans often in minute detail; the L.M.S. actually receiving a request, on one occasion, for Indian troops to break a long journey, one hour in every four, so that they could prepare food and perform religious rituals!

As the war progressed, many towns and districts throughout the country became specialized training centres, and parties of troops had to be conveyed there at intervals. Sometimes whole armoured formations, in armoured fighting vehicle trains carrying from 10 to 18 tanks plus personnel, would travel from the south of England to training grounds in the northern counties of Scotland. The majority of troop movements was, however, made up of small parties of 20 or more, and in 1943 the Company provided accommodation for as many as 51,392 such parties.

Then, too, the build-up of our forces in the Middle East was going on constantly from August, 1940, and at an ever increasing momentum, but the pace quickened in May, 1942, and in November of that year the most extensive draft ever dealt with (until then) was despatched—339 trains being run in 13 days. Incidentally this was the beginning of the movement which eventually sealed the fate of the Germans and Italians in North Africa, and led to the great advances which only finished with the overthrow of their armies in Tunisia the following summer.

As for the departure of any other large convoy, this meant the assembly at ports of tens of thousands of troops of every type and every rank, coming from many scattered camps and depots in England, Scotland, Wales and Northern Ireland, many of them having to be delivered at the docks, together with thousands of tons of supplies, on time-table schedule.

Large-scale military manoeuvres were another feature of railway work at this time, when many units both of the attacking and defending forces had to be taken to their initial battle stations. The return of the "belligerents" at the conclusion of the exercise was often a complex affair, for the tide of battle was uncertain, and the finish could rarely be predicted or foreseen. In order, therefore, to simplify the operational train work, a Central Inter-

Railway Control with special telephones was set up to co-operate with the Military Movement Control in the area concerned. Several of these "battles" took place, and on one occasion 221 trains were called for in a week. The experience gained under these semi-active conditions was invaluable to everyone, especially against the time when the traffic for D-Day would start to roll to the ports in concentrated volume.

Then there was leave. Through these long years of the build-up, leave was going on nearly all the time, and the volume was always difficult to gauge. For example, 71 special trains were required for leave traffic on one day alone, and specials were a regular feature in coping with troops coming from and returning to Northern Ireland, the Orkneys and Shetlands and Iceland.

Periodically, prisoners of war were dealt with. The first special for this particular traffic ran from Thurso in September, 1939, the passengers being the crew of a captured U-boat. In June, 1940, nine specials were in operation on one day, following the Government's decision to transfer prisoners of war from this country to the Dominions. Then in July, 1941, came the first Italians from the Middle East for agricultural work, and after the successful conclusion of the North African campaign, dozens of specials were busy conveying droves more of these unfortunate and misguided people, together with their late German masters, to camps in Scotland, Northumberland, Leicestershire and Gloucestershire.

In October, 1943, the railways had a hand in a small but notable movement. For the first time repatriated British prisoners of war returned home from Germany via Sweden. They landed at Leith and at Liverpool, and though the L.N.E.R. were involved in the major part of this work, several ambulance trains were worked by the L.M.S.

Last, but by no means least, came troops to this country from overseas. The first to reach our shores was a contingent of Canadians who landed in the West of Scotland in December, 1939. Further arrivals followed at intervals—contingents large and small. From 1940 to 1943 they came from all parts of the Empire, and included large numbers of airmen trained under the vast Empire Training Scheme in Canada and the States.

Up to May, 1940, the Clyde alone was used as a disembarkation point for troops from the Dominions and Colonies, but later Liverpool was made use of. Both ports are served largely by the L.M.S., but owing to the shipping position, so precarious and so vitally important at that time, the need for radio silence made it impossible to obtain information of the number of vessels which would be ordered to either of these ports until they were very close to the British Isles. It was essential, therefore, so that troops could be quickly disembarked and moved away by rail, to have plans drawn up providing for trains to leave from either Liverpool or Glasgow—one or both. This meant that no definite train arrangements could be made until the ships had almost docked. The fact that the L.M.S. in Glasgow alone handled (in and out) 3,000,000 service personnel in the war years, 1939–43, will give some indication of the volume of traffic that was passing.

Assuredly service transport had inherent characteristics of its own. There could be no long-term planning as for the Grand National or the England v. Scotland Soccer International. Plans were often made at a moment's notice, and sometimes when the movement was well under way extensive alterations were required in the teeth of enemy air activity.

. . . . .

On January 6th, 1942, this historic message from President Roosevelt to Congress was broadcast to the world:

American land, air and sea forces will take status in the British Isles, which will constitute an essential fortress in this world struggle.

The same day saw the never-to-be-forgotten arrival of U.S. forces in the British Isles, when a substantial number of their troops disembarked in Northern Ireland—they were the welcome vanguard of many more. Much railway transport for our new allies in that country was undertaken by the Northern Counties Committee (a subsidiary of the L.M.S.), and amongst other things, so as to make room for the newcomers, they assisted their parent company to shift an entire army division of British troops across the Irish Sea to the south of England.

When the main body of U.S. troops came to England, Scotland and Wales, they were dealt with largely by the Company. From the Clyde, the Mersey, and the Bristol Channel, hundreds of trainloads fanned out to all parts of the land. The first really big convoy arrived in July, 1943, and required 86 trains before it was cleared. In September, there was a bigger one still—148 trains, but the largest of the lot came in October, no less than 203 specials being run on six consecutive days.

Those, however, were just the peak movements. There were many smaller ones, both in between, before and after. Indeed in November two convoys came into port in quick succession, and the total number of trains dealt with from the west coast during that parti-cular month was 496.

Behind all of the foregoing lies a long story of difficulties overcome, of convoys deflected or delayed, of sudden calls for the rapid entraining of troops from fast unconvoyed ocean liners like the *Queen Mary* and the *Queen Elizabeth*, of the complementary work involved in moving empty coaching stock, of gale and fog, of ice and snow, and of the one-time insistence by the service authorities of "daylight only" disembarkation, which resulted in the loss of many thousands of train hours. Always, too, there was the priority demand for locomotives, rolling stock and train gangs, a demand which was ever on the increase. But somehow the job was successfully accomplished though the devil on countless occasions was pulled severely by the tail.

Four long and weary years they were, in a Britain often battered from above by a ruthless enemy. But a Britain with one constant thought—D-Day—and to get back once more across the Channel at the throat of the Hun. Through those years the railways were the willing horses of the nation and the Allied forces. They had their heads down for every mile of the long journey. It was dirty weather and the way all uphill.

FREIGHT

So much for the transport of troops. What about the movement of equipment, munitions, armour and food for the fighting man himself? His requirements were almost endless in variety and number, and apart from his everyday needs a surplus had to be built up to cover all emergencies, losses, and misfortunes from Acts of God to the King's Enemies.

There was porridge for his breakfast, shells for his guns and boots for his feet—beer to bull-dozers, pencils to purgatives, saucepans to cement, together with special equipment for service anywhere from the Arctic Circle to the tropic jungles, or from the near stratosphere to the depths of the sea. So far as the railways were concerned, these had to be drawn to or from the ports and also from place to place within the country.

At the beginning of the war, with the nation's main fighting forces in France, the job was simple enough and entailed the regular despatch of a few trainloads a week. But as the Allied forces were built up in the Middle East, and as the number of servicemen and women increased in Great Britain, the task became a formidable one.

Generally speaking, the various service departments kept their supplies and munitions in depots. There were hundreds of them. The War Office, for instance, had stores in all parts of the country—the vast majority situated in the West, with the result that the continual and increasing transfer of stocks from factory to depot and from depot to the ports (and vice versa) was largely an L.M.S. affair. In fact some 70 per cent of the 8,000 standard journeys available (any one of which could be called for by a short and simple code, and at a moment's notice) were routed over the Company's system.

This traffic was not always a matter of supplying wagons and drawing the supplies from place to place. Take tanks for example. Tank designs in the early months of the war were frequently modified, and alterations did not always take into account the fact that unless dimensions were kept within the limits of ordinary railway requirements, special "out of gauge" precautions were necessary. This restricted not only the speed, but the actual routes on which the trains could travel, so that railway structures or trains moving in the opposite direction should not be fouled.

A particular case arose over tanks sent to the Libyan Desert. After the first experience of fighting there, tank designers decided to fix sand-shields over the tracks of the next consignments, but it was overlooked that these shields fouled the loading gauge, and as a consequence a much slower and circuitous journey had to be made.

Such difficulties were further increased in 1943 when the factories had really got into their stride. Indeed in that year there were more than 10,000 "out of gauge" loads which included huge transformers, guns and the parts of ships.

Much ingenuity had to be exercised in the use and adaptation of wagons for the conveyance of war material of exceptional dimensions. One novel expedient evolved by the operating department concerned the conveyance of aeroplane propellers. The enormous number eventually passing by rail soon made it impossible to provide sufficient of the special type vehicles required. High sided wagons, therefore, were converted by removal of the four centre floor planks, so that one arm of the propeller could be dropped into this aperture, and the two other arms supported in the wagon itself by means of wooden cradles. A practice, incidentally, which later on was adopted by all the railway companies.

But even when trains reached the docks there was never any absolute certainty that their goods would be taken aboard; sometimes, too, and owing to lack of shipping space, there was congestion at the vessel's side when the stuff had to be returned to the ordnance depots without being moved from their wagons. Special care and vigilance was, of course, always necessary to see that trains turned up at the ports in proper sequence. Dockers are men who command an extensive vocabulary, and when a trainload of tanks for bottom loading arrived after light cases for top loading, they were not sparing in making use of it.

Flexibility of planning and initiative on the part of the railways were very important factors in getting the ships turned round quickly. One little-known piece of train work for shipment overseas was undertaken when Germany declared war on Russia in June, 1941. The British Government immediately announced that full material support would be given to our new allies, and a couple of months later, between August and November, the following specials were despatched largely by L.M.S.:

Above—1939: half a million schoolchildren evacuated in four days
Below—The roof-spotter keeps watch

Day in, day out, the main-line stations of the L.M.S. saw such scenes as this

Above—From Stranraer Harbour, train ferries carried streams of war material to Northern Ireland

Below—Tanks loaded on "Warwells" being marshalled by an Army shunter

Above—General Winter in command

Below—An evening scene. Difficulties of marshalling and despatching freight trains were immeasurably increased by the blackout

Aluminium	..	..	..	8
Rubber..	..	..	..	30
Clothing	..	..	..	8
Boots ..	..	..	..	37
Sugar ..	..	..	..	13
Cocoa ..	..	..	..	2
Copper and zinc..	..	..	3
Bombs	..	..	..	3
Tanks and carriers		..	..	28

———

132

It was an amazing contribution at that stage of the war from a country which had so recently stood alone, and which had then suffered, and was still suffering extensive damage from aerial bombardment. But "Go To It" and "Britain Delivers The Goods" were then the popular slogans of the day.

During the course of the war, urgent consignments of stores and equipment were often required at the ports in a special hurry so that the sailing time of a ship should not be delayed. One typical case is referred to in an L.M.S. operating department report. The train involved was a special of 34 wagons from Woolwich to Glasgow.

> The L.M.S. was told that a heavy naval gun with its component parts was loaded up and would be leaving a depot on the outskirts of London for exchange to the L.M.S. at the nearest junction in five hours time, whence it was to be worked forward by special train to Clydeside, to arrive there within 38 hours. The train consisted of nine wagons of special type which could not be worked at high speed, also eight ordinary goods wagons. Incidentally, the train was exchanged four hours later than anticipated, so that the L.M.S. had a period of 29 hours in which to run the slow-moving train a distance of 400 miles, over what can be claimed as the busiest route in Great Britain. However, the staff rose to the occasion and the gun reached its destination five hours within the time limit, thus travelling 400 miles in 24 hours. . . .

Over and above the despatch of train specials to the ports, there was a vast and increasing amount of haulage work within the country. Munitions, for instance, from factories to storage depots, and as further depots were established, redistribution from depot to depot.

The working of this traffic did not, however, present any real difficulties, as prior notice could generally be given. But there was much cross haulage from the south to the north and vice versa, and the burden to the railways would have been eased considerably if the ports nearest the depots or factories had been used. Although it was recognized that this could not always be done, cross haulage became so extensive in 1942 that special representations were made to the War Office, and examples given of how rail transport could have been saved.

So the volume of freight for the services grew and grew. Indeed in 1943, 400 special L.M.S. trains and more, were often run in a single week, and in addition many thousands of wagons, especially for the maintenance of our armies abroad, were despatched by the railway's ordinary trains. It is safe to say that every freight train of the Company was conveying one or more such wagons, and special facilities were arranged for transfer from one train to another—sometimes four or five exchanges being necessary in a long and complicated journey.

The work undertaken for the different war departments was full of variety, and the stuff of war sped over the lines in colossal quantities. There were explosives, bombs, grenades, shells and chemical defence preparations—there was barbed wire—indeed up to June, 1942, the Company ran 760 special trains conveying 5,000,000 coils of barbed wire from *a single factory* in the north-west area alone. Then there was petrol. In August and September, 1943, when our bombing offensive had reached new heights, and before the pipe lines came into full use, no less than 200 special trains, conveying well over 20,000,000 gallons of fuel, were run weekly over the L.M.S. system. This was largely a haulage from ports in the west to aerodromes in the east—from the Mersey and the Severn to bomber bases in Lincoln and East Anglia.

Each time we raided the enemy on the Continent, several trainloads of petrol were sent off to air bases to replenish depleted stocks.

Although this was one of the railway's major achievements in the nation's war effort, there were many other sinews of war besides petrol that were carried *from* the ports. Merchant ships arrived with ever-increasing frequency, and hurriedly discharged their cargo to return for more. The flow was unending, and included raw commodities, finished articles and food from our Empire and foreign countries—the welcome products of lease-lend, and latterly, of stores and food and munitions for the vast needs of the U.S.A. troops in Great Britain.

When it was decided to build up a powerful American army and air force in the country, the whole question of supplies became one of major importance. It being manifestly impossible for this country to cover their requirements, inasmuch as our production was not adequate for our own needs—nearly everything necessary to feed, clothe, furnish, equip and munition our allies had to be imported, mostly, of course, from across the Atlantic.

The material commenced to pass in quantity in August, 1942, and its growth was rapid. In September–December, 1942, for instance, 22,956 wagon loads were forwarded from L.M.S. *ports*, but in the same four months of 1943 it had risen to 36,914, and in addition there was much depot to depot work.

The first essential was to see that ships which arrived in convoy from the States were loaded as far as possible with cargo destined for the same part of the country, and consigned to a port conveniently placed to serve that area. For this purpose railway officials were sent to America to advise shipping agents there how best this might be achieved in order to obtain short hauls and avoid cross haulage after unloading at our ports.

A very effective and close collaboration was soon established with the American authorities, not only in the States, but throughout Great Britain, both at the docks and on the railways.

Some impression of the magnitude of the task performed by the Company's operating department on behalf of the services to May 8th, 1945 (VE-Day), will be found in the following figures:

PASSENGER TRAINS RUN

Special trains	..	..	89,926	Baggage, tons	.. ..	531,099
Officers conveyed	..	..	949,084	Horses	.. ..	47,225
Other ranks	..	..	25,552,183			

FREIGHT TRAINS RUN

Equipment and Stores

Special trains	.. ..	49,141
Wagons conveyed	..	1,758,947

Petrol

Special trains	.. ..	27,043
Tank wagons conveyed	..	747,558
Gallons conveyed (approx.)		2,704,300,000

Ammunition

Special trains	.. ..	11,253
Number of wagons	..	396,411

Forces Mail

Special trains	.. ..	2,621
Wagons conveyed	.. ..	42,612

In the words of Mark Twain the work was "interesting but tough." Well might it be said that the railways were the fourth arm of the services.

CHAPTER SIX

THE WEATHER OFFENSIVE

THE railways had to put up with several different offensives during the war. They ranged from the H.E. bombs of the German Air Force to the terse expletives of delayed and irritable passengers. But of them all, snow, frost and blizzard often had the most paralysing and widespread effects, and in the first three winters weather conditions were at times without modern precedent.

It has been said that an examination of meteorological statistics will show a tendency for a specially cold spell to visit Great Britain in cycles of 45 years. If this is so, the country was due for some such recurrence, and it got it. In many districts the weather was the worst of the century, with recordings of the lowest temperatures, and the heaviest falls of snow. There was only one compensation. The fog offensive was not so prevalent as in milder winters, but where fog of itself can only delay the railways, snow and frost can hold them up altogether.

In the first winter of the war there was considerable fog in December, and this, coupled with particularly heavy rail traffic at Christmas, left considerable arrears to be cleared up. Before this could be done, however, heavy falls of snow were succeeded by prolonged frost, and a climax reached between January 27th and 29th, 1940, when snowstorms and blizzards attained such ferocity that conditions were soon so appalling they couldn't have been worse.

On the L.M.S. system alone, there were 313 separate snow blocks, sometimes 20 feet deep, with the result that many trains and engines were stuck fast in various parts of the country, 250 telegraph poles blown down, and 500 miles of telegraph and telephone wires put out of action.

In the words of the Railway Executive Committee's report: "everything that could freeze froze." Points seized, and brake gear of freight trains became immovable, signal wires jammed or snapped, engine injectors froze, grease in the axle boxes solidified and couplings had to be hammered apart.

The effect was widespread, for scores of marshalling yards ceased to function, and goods station freight could not be cleared owing to the state of the roads. Hotels were short of food, steamers delayed, passengers stranded, and coal, which could normally be tipped, had to be hacked from the wagons with a pick.

Snow fell practically throughout the vast L.M.S. system. There were few areas north of Glasgow not deeply affected, while things were particularly severe in the areas Rugby–Kettering and Largs–Carstairs. Traffic movement over approximately a thousand miles of the line was either brought to a standstill or considerably delayed, and even on the main lines where eight trains would normally pass every hour, there were no through expresses for seven days.

One train which left Glasgow for Euston on the first of these seven days, a Saturday, did not get to London until Tuesday, while three express trains which left the same terminus a little later were brought to a standstill near the 1,000-foot Beattock Summit; some of the passengers having to shelter in the neighbouring villages for five days.

It was all something of a nightmare, and the hold-up to industry, and the war effort generally, was really serious. Especially so was this the case with coal, for hundreds of collieries were cut off from rail access, and thousands of empty wagons immobilized.

Wherever possible the Company immediately put clearing gangs and snow ploughs into action. One snow block between Lancaster and Preston took an army of workers four days to free, but sometimes the rescue trains themselves became snowed up, and the snow ploughs bogged. As if this were not enough, the thaw added a new set of complications. There were many serious landslides, and the lines were again blocked. Indeed in one place it was 26 days before 10,000 tons of rock and soil could be moved, and traffic was again free to pass.

Through it all the staff worked hard to try and set matters to rights, but in the end many thousands fell ill, and small wonder after what they had gone through. In a general tot-up in the middle of February, it was found that of train crews alone, 9 per cent of the Company's engine drivers and firemen and 13 per cent of the guards were on the sick list, mainly with influenza.

Yet in spite of these Job-like visitations, only in one of the first eight weeks of 1940 was the movement of freight traffic less than for the same period in 1939, the railway actually running an additional 11,500,000 loaded wagon miles. In the face of everything it was a herculean effort.

Although conditions in the next winter (1940–41) were not so severe, the weather was again abnormal. Heavy snowstorms occurred in many parts of the country between January 18th and 30th, and in Lancashire and Yorkshire and the north of Scotland they continued up to February 8th. Lines were again blocked in 76 recorded places, and many trains stuck or derailed in drifts. 5,000 troops were employed assisting the Company in clearing the lines. Outstanding difficulties occurred on the single line to Thurso—of such vital importance during the war—and several H.M. Forces trains were diverted elsewhere, and the men billeted until conditions grew less severe.

Some idea of what the Company's staff had to face in this particular area will be seen in the following extract from *Carry On*, the L.M.S. house magazine.

> In the vicinity of Forsinard and Altnabreac, about 130 miles north of Inverness (a region notorious for severe snow blockages in the past), two freight trains were completely snowed up for three days. A snow plough sent from Wick to clear the line became itself snowed up at Altnabreac, and the P.W. Inspector and 52 men who had gone to clear the line were isolated. Flying across snowy wastes under appalling weather conditions an aeroplane (R.A.F.) succeeded in dropping supplies of food for the marooned men, who were fortunately able to get their train out soon afterwards, being assisted by a "relief" from Inverness carrying fresh men and equipment.

An R.A.F. plane was again employed in the district some days later on, when food was dropped for 90 passengers and 62 permanent way men isolated at three separate places. And on another occasion a loaded restaurant car was sent to feed both passengers and crew until they could proceed on their journey.

On the law of averages it might have been thought that the next winter (1941–42), things would have been easier, but it was not to be. For the third season running, the weather was again extreme. It is another long story of lines blocked and passengers and freight storm-bound. To add to the difficulties, points became fixed. This was general along and west of the line Birmingham to Glasgow, where fine powdery snow sealed them up as fast as they could be released.

At the height of the blizzard, everyone available, including the staff and soldiers from neighbouring camps and towns, was hard at work fighting a heartbreaking battle. To start with, it was no mean task finding these points, covered as they often were by 3 feet of snow, and when it is appreciated that at Crewe, to take but one place of many, there are over 200 pairs of points—the difficulties can be imagined.

Notwithstanding the fact that so many passenger trains were held up in snowdrifts, no travellers were injured, and somehow or other it was always possible for them to find food or accommodation in the vicinity. The only serious case occurred between Kinbrace and Forsinard, when the 11.40 a.m. military special from Keith to Wick became stuck in a snowdrift during the early morning of January 25th, and was not cleared until the afternoon of the 27th. Food, however, was again dropped by aeroplane, and the men released on the 28th.

During those three wild winters, much uninformed criticism of the railways was worked off by the travelling public (part of the expletive offensive) for the effect was often felt well away from the area affected; people in the south having no conception of what was going on in the north. It was particularly galling for the railwayman to have to listen to it all. He had made tremendous efforts not only against the elements, but in trying to fight down attacks of sickness when by rights he should have been in bed. And listen was all he could do, being unable to explain just what was going on elsewhere because of the rigorous censorship on weather reports.

Like Kipling's cat he was "waving his wild tail and walking by his wild lone. But he never told anybody." And when he could tell anybody after the lawful number of days had elapsed—no one was the least bit interested!

CHAPTER SEVEN

CIVILIAN PASSENGER TRAFFIC

S OME account has been given of the work which the railways did for the services from 1939 to VE-Day. It was a big job, but the work done for the civilian and the factories was far greater. War meant upheaval in nearly every sphere of life. It came banging at castle gate and cottage door—men and women joined the services, and the nation began to play a huge game of general post. The petrol pump attendant went to drive a tractor on the farm, the caddie master at the golf club returned to his old love the fishing fleet, the middle-aged tobacconist and confectioner shut up his little village shop and got a temporary job in the Civil Service, the lift girl in the multiple stores became a nurse in the city hospital.

Engineers who once constructed motor-cars constructed tanks, and women who once made silk stockings made munitions. New factories were built, sleepy villages suddenly became alive with industry, forests were felled, mines re-opened. The anvils of the gods of war rang from one end of the country to the other, and the united pre-war family was soon scattered to the four points of the compass.

Early in 1939 the railways were faced with the job of foreseeing the alterations that would be required in the face of these changes, and a beginning was made in the production of a wartime passenger time-table. Air raids and the demands of the forces were of course a cardinal consideration, with the result that the ordinary peacetime trains had to be pared down, and arrangements made for the suspension of dining cars and sleepers, and also for the reduction of train speeds (safety measure) in order to keep within a maximum average of 45 m.p.h. between stops.

This involved not only a colossal amount of work inside the L.M.S. offices, but constant collaboration and extensive planning with the other main-line companies. Indeed, this inter-company collaboration was a remarkable and successful feature of all wartime railway work, and great economies in the saving of train miles and man-power were brought about.

These war time-tables had been completed in July, 1939, and on Monday, September 11th, they were brought into force. On the whole a pretty good shot had been made at foreseeing the new order. It was only natural, however, that some adjustments would have to be made and services augmented where experience showed this to be necessary. Gradually, too, several items were improved—dining-cars and sleepers* re-introduced, and acceleration of main-line and secondary services became general over the entire system.

It was, however, a difficult period and continual vigilance had to be kept on all movements. On the cessation of Summer Time, for instance, in the first war winter, the earlier blackout made many business houses and offices alter their hours of work with a view to staffs getting home before dark. This meant that the evening rush hour started and finished an hour earlier, and the morning peak period telescoped from two to one and a half hours. Workmen's trains were another special feature of the altered conditions, for not only were

---

* In order to increase carrying capacity and to discourage other than essential passenger travel, all but 28 restaurant cars were withdrawn in May, 1942, and these came off in April, 1944. At the same time sleeping car accommodation on certain heavily loaded trains was taken over by the Ministry of War Transport and limited so that first call on sleeping berths was given to passengers travelling on urgent Government business.

factories more distributed throughout the country (often where there was little or no living accommodation), but the step-up of the industrial effort to include night shifts, seven days a week, involved the moving of a large number of additional trains. On the L.M.S. these ran into thousands; at Chorley (Lancs.) to cite but one case, 222,500 journeys were made each week by factory workers alone. But by the beginning of 1940 all time-tables had been so arranged that they could be more or less maintained with special adjustments to meet specific demands.

Naturally enough the high standard of peacetime travel could not be upheld. The flow of traffic was uncertain, trains were sometimes unpunctual and often overcrowded. The public groused; but in spite of everything—the attenuated service, the blackout, air raids and so on—the Company did its best. As Lord Castlerosse once said: "England expects the railways to do their duty and the impossible."

As far as unpunctuality went, the blackout was the chief offender. There were delays in entraining and detraining. Passengers had difficulty in finding seats when blinds were drawn. Soldiers carried bulky kit, retarding movements through corridors and doorways. Apart from the passengers, however, trains had to convey much more luggage, parcels, post and mails, together with Government traffic of weights far exceeding those carried under normal conditions. The loading and unloading of all these in the restricted lighting took far more time than normally. And over and above everything, there was the paramount necessity of keeping down the number of passengers and parcels to the smallest practical volume in order to conserve man-power and engines, and to relieve the lines to the fullest capacity for the transport of the materials of war.

Another difficulty the railways had to meet in trying to keep their trains punctual was the reduction of staff due to call-ups to the forces, and their replacement by less able-bodied men, and latterly by women, who, though manfully doing their best could not always be expected to handle heavy and bulky packages with equal speed.

In one way or another, therefore, the railways had a hard row to hoe, and there are 15 major points in the operating department's reports, explaining why the punctuality of passenger trains could not always be maintained. They extend from increased engine failures to excessive hauls, and from air raid warning delays to inferior coal.

As long as the war lasted it was impossible to remove most of these troubles, but in order to bring about as high a degree of punctuality as was possible, no stone was left unturned. Improvements were obtained in the lighting at stations and in the brake vans, speeds were raised wherever possible, additional trains were run exclusively for parcels, staff travelled on board sorting packages en route, loudspeakers were installed to assist passengers in stations, and advice and help were provided by travelling ticket collectors, who also tried to see that passengers were ready to alight at their proper destinations.

By comparison with the 1914–18 war, when there were no blackout or air raids as now known, the position compared not unfavourably, and the decrease in passenger trains, punctual or not less than five minutes late, ranged from only 1 to 2 per cent.

.   .   .   .

Holiday traffic was another major problem of civilian rail traffic. As has already been mentioned, 73 trains were required in one day alone for servicemen's leave. This was on December 21st, 1939, and the total extra trains run on the last 13 days of that month, for

L.M.S. EXPRESS BOMBED AND MACHINE-GUNNED NEAR BLETCHLEY. OCTOBER, 1940

the forces, was 385. But for civilians in the same period no less than 2,693 were required, with a peak day on the 23rd, of 644.

As a result of this—the first general holiday season of the war—the matter had to be taken in hand, and for the future everything was done to try and alleviate the railways' position. The services were approached and agreed to help, while the Minister of War Transport appealed to the public not to travel unless it was absolutely essential. At Christmas, 1940, the Railway Executive Committee issued an announcement to the effect that the Government required the railways to use all their resources for the movement of traffic essential to the nation's war effort, and there would be no additional services or cheap travel.

All this had some effect, and there was a considerable easing off, but travel was still heavy and often necessitated duplicate trains in order to help many people who were stranded. Followed blast and counter-blast. The matter was a vexed one, and in this affair the railways were in the position of being placed in the wrong whatever they did, for if they had failed to run extra trains to cater for passengers who were left high and dry at intermediate stops or junctions, chaotic conditions would have arisen.

In 1941 the public were again enjoined to spend their holidays without travelling. Easter passed without any undue pressure, but at Whitsuntide, heavy passenger traffic was on the move again, especially in the industrial north, where many workers had had no holiday since the beginning of the war, and mental anxiety, nervous strain and disturbed rest were beginning to tell.

The Government recognized this in the summer with provision for a break, but during the year a further campaign was made in the Press and on the wireless to discourage railway travel. The Railway Executive Committee issued posters and advertisements in different forms, and various conscience-pricking phrases spread by this medium through the land.

But *still*, traffic was heavy, and doubtless there were many arguments 'twixt a man's better self and his worse, that surely just one more wouldn't make any difference. But when that one more was multiplied time and again there could be only one result!

And so it went on—a national "stay at home" holidays campaign was launched in 1942, but even so, there was again a spate of travel. During May—September inclusive, passenger journeys in the long-distance categories rose to new heights. In total they exceeded the corresponding figures for 1938 by 74 per cent; and, be it noted that inordinately heavy traffic was carried concurrently with record movements of service personnel travelling on duty or leave.

Those appeals to restrict passenger traffic were, in the main, not very successful. There could be no doubt that the public suffering more and more from the strain of years of intensive war effort, and having the advantage of a higher remuneration for their labours, felt justified in seeking relaxation in pleasure, or paying visits to their own families and relations back home.

In March, 1943, the Ministry of Production requested industry to see that everything possible be done to stagger holidays (an attempt had been made previously), and the Minister of War Transport laid down a policy for the running of additional passenger trains during the summer. These, however, were still more or less restricted to the level of 1942, and with the further increase in travel for the year, the railways found it extremely difficult to anticipate and legislate for overcrowding.

Disregard of the appeal to take advantage of "stay at home" holidays is illustrated in the flow of traffic during the holiday period, May–September, to the Blackpool district:

The total journeys were as follows:

1938 .. 2,426,248   1942 .. 2,068,682   1943 .. 2,598,600

It must be admitted, that with a lot of tolerance and even more good humour John Bull put up with a good deal. On occasions he was in much the same plight as the proverbial sardine, and the national Press represented him in joke drawings and cartoons hanging on to the outside of his coach, and even running patriotically beside it. He was, however, a brave railwayman who defended overcrowding by saying: "Don't you know there's a war on, Sir?" But somehow the job was done, and few, if any, ever failed to reach their destinations.

In the middle of it all the railways derived some comfort from the following message sent to them by the Minister of War Transport:

> Over the August Bank Holiday, 1943, as well as the previous week-end, the strength and ingenuity of all those engaged in the operation of trains and buses was taxed to the utmost, and it is to their credit the situation was kept well under control. Lord Leathers congratulates transport staffs generally—not least the women—on the successful and efficient way in which they tackled a difficult situation.
>
> It should not be forgotten that the passenger on the platform sees only one side of the railwayman's work. The more important work goes on behind the scenes in the depots, sidings and offices; and thanks to the devotion to duty shown by the staffs everywhere the flow of traffic essential to our fighting forces was successfully maintained. In offering his congratulations to the transport personnel, Lord Leathers wishes to thank all those members of the public who wisely refrained from travelling. They chose the better part.

One little-known side of the L.M.S. passenger service was the journeys made during the war by Their Majesties the King and Queen. For these, the Company's Royal Train was used, and in one way or another, up to end of 1944 no fewer than 57 tours were completed on the Company's system, covering 31,127 miles.

This Royal Train is a sort of travelling hotel with facilities for both day and night travel, and it enabled Their Majesties and their entourage to pay visits in all parts of the country, without having to rely on any other accommodation. In this manner they visited many establishments of the Fleet, Army and Air Force, munition factories and ordnance depots; and those many areas stricken by enemy air attacks.

Most of these tours lasted several days, and meals and rest were taken on board, while at night, with the railway police on guard, the most elaborate precautions were made against the risk of enemy action, and the train stabled, when practicable, near a tunnel into which it could be drawn in the event of an air raid. For security reasons the utmost secrecy was preserved, and no mention was made in advices to the line that the King and Queen would be travelling.

The L.M.S. Royal Train was also loaned to other companies during the war as under:

L.N.E.R. .. 44 tours   G.W.R. .. 13 tours   S.R. .. 6 tours

In addition to the Royal Train the railways were also asked to give exceptional travel facilities to many prominent public officials and senior members of the fighting forces, so that journeys could be undertaken under conditions of privacy and secrecy.

The special train for the Prime Minister, for instance, was provided by the L.M.S., the vehicles set aside being a first-class brake, two saloons, a first-class vestibule, first-class dining car, sleeping cars, etc., one saloon being specially adapted for the Prime Minister's personal use. The Company also undertook all catering, and the requisite staff travelled with the train, whether on its own system or that of other companies.

. . . . .

In one way or another, therefore, civilian passenger traffic was a very big feature indeed of the L.M.S. at war, with further ramifications extending from the carriage of racing pigeons to the transport of Christmas mail for the American forces, which, in 1943, ran to 168,613 bags.

But the biggest demands came through the increased labour demand of industry. On the main-line railways when unemployment figures had dropped to negligible proportions, journeys at workmen's fares increased in provincial centres by as much as 70 per cent.

Some relief was, however, obtained by the staggering of working hours, so as to provide a more even flow of traffic both to and from the factories. But the burden was always heavy.

CIVILIAN AND FACTORY FREIGHT

In the average British home there are very few articles which have not at one time or another been carried by train—furniture, food, fuel, clothes, china, carpets, even the bricks and mortar of the building itself. It is the same with the nation as a whole, its factories, its shops, its fisheries, its farms.

The part which the railways played during the war in what the railwayman calls "freight operating" was colossal. In 1943 on the L.M.S. system alone 370,100 loaded wagons were being forwarded every week, and by comparison with the 1938 figures the additional miles covered amounted to 190,900 per week.

Although much planning had been done for the moving of goods in anticipation of an outbreak of hostilities, no fundamental changes were made prior to September, 1939, and even with the advent of war (unlike the passenger services), there were no drastic alterations in the running of the trains. The arranging of emergency time-tables was not considered practicable, because the problems to be faced were not only uncertain but in the main unknown. The one salient feature that could be envisaged was the fact that the volume of freight would increase as the war effort gained momentum, and as traffic was diverted from road vehicles and coastwise shipping.

It gradually became clear, however, that trains would have to run at slower speeds, and carry heavier loads—that the flows of traffic would change and extend, that there would be a retardation in clearing wagons from the goods yards, due to the blackout, and that there must of necessity be a general slowing up in the already well-filled lines on account of mobilization, special trains, and all the priority demands of the services and Government.

The 1939 summer time-table of the Company was, therefore, continued, and altered when necessary to meet the changing conditions, and as many trains as possible started on their journeys during daylight in an endeavour to avoid the pernicious influence of the blackout. This in itself meant a lengthening of transit hours, for in peacetime a large proportion of freight traffic is on the move at night, the goods being loaded up after collection in the late afternoon and conveyed to distant centres in time for delivery the following morning.

However, once the passenger train services had reached a comparatively settled state, the requirements of freight traffic could be measured with a degree of accuracy sufficient to bring out a revised working time-table, and this was done in February, 1940, subsequent revisions being made as they became necessary.

One of the outstanding features of railway working during the war was the vast variations in the flow of freight traffic, the character and intensity of which introduced many novel problems. For it must be remembered that although the country is very well covered in the matter of railway lines, they had developed under private enterprise, and unlike Germany, for example, were not basically constructed with a military and strategic background. In other words, British railways were laid out for the movement of traffic in well defined flows dictated by peacetime considerations, so that revolutionary changes in the nature of the war work they were required to perform were inevitable—and especially was this so in view of the unexpected turn of events due to Dunkirk.

Radical alterations in the flow and volume soon began to disclose bottlenecks, and superimposed on all this was the effect of the enormous increase in the use of the west coast ports, and the bunching which resulted from the use of the convoy system. Another prominent feature in the altered volume and flow of freight was soon made manifest by the building and establishment of numerous new factories and depots, and by the strategic policy of decentralizing these away from congested and vulnerable areas—especially the large towns. This meant that hundreds of quiet country spots, many on branch lines or on minor cross-country rail routes, became intensive centres of industry.

Everywhere there were rail problems both complex and new. To take one specific type of freight—coal. In peacetime a large proportion of the nation's coal was carried by sea from one coast port to another, but with the arrival of the enemy on the coasts of Holland, Belgium and France, the sea route around the east and south coasts of England became too hazardous.

In normal times coal from Northumberland and Durham was largely conveyed by the railways only for the short journey between the collieries and the north-east coast ports, where it was shipped either abroad or sent by coasters to London and the south and south-west ports. The new conditions entailed vast quantities of this same coal being taken lengthy distances by rail not only to London, but often as far as Devon and Cornwall. Coal from Wales, normally exported, also flowed to inland destinations.

Much was done to alleviate the position by the running of "block" trains, i.e., full trainloads from a colliery direct to one destination or group of destinations, thus obviating shunting and reshunting in the marshalling yards en route. But even so, the additional burden to the railways was enormous, for eventually they were carrying 4,000,000 tons weekly, amounting to some 80 per cent of the country's saleable coal, and of those 4,000,000 tons the L.M.S. conveyed 1,450,000 tons.

Indeed coal was a source of considerable worry, not only to the railways, but the nation as a whole. The publication *Facts About British Railways in Wartime*, 1942, sums the matter up thus:

> In the early part of the war the need for man-power for the fighting forces was paramount. Many colliery workers eagerly answered the call to the colours, with the result that the production of coal fell considerably. During the spring and summer of 1941 men were released from the army and called back from other occupations to return to the collieries to meet the supreme need of supplying war factories with coal.
>
> Unfortunately these men did not return early enough to produce the coal during the

months with long daylight hours, but the output increased in the autumn and winter. As a result, stocks of coal were 3,000,000 tons larger than a year previously, but these vast extra quantities were moved by the railways which were already heavily engaged carrying munitions, raw materials and the hundred and one things called for by a nation at war.

Again, it is unnecessary to emphasize the importance of iron ore, and the demand for steel in mechanized warfare, but this was another commodity which developed a new and additional flow as the battle progressed. Prior to the war a large proportion of Great Britain's iron ore was imported from abroad, as it was richer than that mined at home, and for this reason most blast furnaces will be found within easy reach of the ports. The war, of course, stopped most sources of foreign supply, and this necessitated a large expansion of home-produced ore.

In spite of many difficulties, however, iron ore was moved with comparative smoothness by the railways, largely to the north-east of England, and to the Scottish blast furnaces —and, owing to the geographical position of these quarries in the South and East Midlands, the L.M.S. shouldered yet one more heavy burden in its movement.

So far as freight traffic generally is concerned, the railwayman divides it into three main classes: (a) coal, (b) other minerals (including iron ore), and (c) merchandise.

The last involves a considerable amount of operating effort, as it embraces all raw materials except coal, coke, iron ore, limestone, etc. Indeed it includes nearly everything else imaginable—bales of wool, timber, cement—anything, in fact, from a small consignment of cigars to a pantechnicon, guinea pigs to cattle, torch batteries to huge electric stators, air gun pellets to 4,000 lb. bombs, tins of mustard to vast consignments of wheat.

The increase in the production of home grown produce and its conveyance by the railways was a major war effort in itself, embracing as it did, potatoes, sugar beet, tractors, and fertilizers, and so far as the L.M.S. was concerned, it was the same with fish and meat. Then there was Scottish timber, the cutting of which had increased to such an extent that in 1943 the tonnage carried by rail rose to 1,513,785 tons, with the L.M.S. conveying the major load.

While this (class (c)) merchandise traffic does not represent the heaviest hauls, it requires, owing to its bulky character in relation to its weight, a much greater number of wagons compared with, say, coal or minerals.

It is, too, a class of traffic which rarely lends itself to transit in trainloads of one commodity like coal, and generally speaking numerous different consignments go to make up a wagon load. Again, though these consignments are sorted and loaded in wagons so as to provide the largest number of *direct* trainloads between two points (thus obviating shunting en route), there is much that does not admit of such treatment.

The movement of part of this particular traffic was, however, reduced as time went on. After the outbreak of war trade conditions were fairly normal, and general merchandise passed much as usual, but as time went on the Government soon recognized that if Britain was to survive, the austere condition of total war must be shouldered by everyone, and that commodities available to the nation as a whole must be reduced to the bare necessities of life, so that maximum man-power could be applied to essential war needs.

This was accomplished by food and clothes rationing, and by the fixing of quotas for the manufacture and sale of goods. The demand for articles was discouraged by purchase tax, and a policy adopted of zoning the distribution of many commodities such as biscuits, fruit, fish and vegetables. The latter was a project advocated by the railways, and it had a marked effect in the elimination of much wasteful rail traffic—6,000 train miles *per week* being actually saved by the fish zoning scheme alone.

Thus it was that gradually, bit by bit, austerity living was introduced to the nation, and by 1942 it had become well and truly established.

.　　　.　　　.　　　.　　　.

Marshalling yards have been referred to in previous chapters. The name was not a very familiar one to the public until our Air Force became busy on the Continent of Europe, and the Press and wireless reported devastating attacks on such large railway centres as Hanover, Cologne and Hamm.

Marshalling yards, as we now know, are large areas of sidings (the one at Basford—south of Crewe—has no less than 22 miles of them, and it is not the biggest) where freight trains made up of wagons for different destinations come to be split up and remade into trains with a common destination or destinations along one particular line or lines. Their function is in fact rather like a sorting place for Post Office letters and parcels.

To the layman marshalling yards will always remain something of a mystery. They are little worlds of their own, presided over by a yard master, whose cares, worries and responsibilities seem to be never-ending. A hundred *starting* freight trains, a hundred *terminating* freight trains and a hundred *through* freight trains are quite an ordinary daily occurrence in his life.

Look at the scene in one of the bigger yards from the elevation of a railway footbridge. Down below on all sides a dozen shunting engines can be seen chivvying and nosing hundreds of wagons about the sidings. Some of these wagons are moved separately, some in groups of twos and threes, until gradually train after train disappears, while others are built up close by with each wagon in the correct order for uncoupling at its allotted station on the next or final stage of the journey.

And again, like so many other railway undertakings, successful working here is largely a matter of control—with yard inspectors, yard foremen, engine drivers, firemen, signalmen, guards, shunters and many others working as a team—their main objective to get the goods through.

But though there is much noise in the marshalling yards—the gruff puffing of steam engines, the throb of the 350 h.p. diesels, the banging and clattering of wagon bumping wagon down the long length of a siding—the human voice is rarely heard. In point of fact, the only apparent communication between those men who are actually in contact control of the wagons on the lines—and they of all railwaymen would seem to have cause to shout their orders and directions—is just a mystical tick-tack of sign and countersign.

Marshalling yards are indeed uncanny places where the layman might well wonder just why things rarely if ever go wrong. For the work is hard and often dangerous, work where a man must have a cool head and be constantly on the lookout for trouble.

The District Controller, in speaking about one such marshalling yard under his charge, admitted: "We don't stop for rain here," adding "My boys have done a tremendous war job, and though Hitler bumped us once or twice he never stopped us working for more than three-quarters of an hour."

The Company's marshalling yards continued to work throughout the war much as they did in peacetime—but many closed yards were opened up, additional ones built and sidings put down at new points to cater for that ever-increasing war traffic.

Many of the larger yards and particularly those dealing with coal and empty mineral wagons, were relieved to some extent by the working of block trains. But this relief was more than counter-balanced by the additional volume of traffic, the slowing down of movement due to the blackout, and the exceptional weather conditions of the first three winters of the war.

In the account of freight work for the services, out-of-gauge and exceptional loads were mentioned. One more such may be described here. The conveyance of the largest, heaviest and most remarkable load ever moved by the British railways. It was accomplished in May, 1941, by the L.M.S. and L.N.E.R. together.

The operating report reads as follows:

> The consignment consisted of a stator weighing 130 tons, from Newcastle to Coleshill via Egginton. The stator, which could only be moved on Sundays and necessitated five weeks to complete the journey, was carried slung on the girders of an L.N.E.R. transformer set fitted with a cantilever arrangement 13 ft. 1½ in. wide, the girders being set in rails to enable the load to be moved transversely 12 in. from centre to either side to clear structures.
>
> A second stator of similar dimensions was later conveyed between the same points.

The main work of the Company's freight operations was, however, largely uninteresting—just a matter of keeping wagon load after wagon load—millions and millions in a single year—on the move and filled to capacity.

In 1943 the position was such that 43 per cent of all loaded wagons forwarded by the railways originated on the L.M.S., while a large quantity of traffic originating on the other railways also passed on to or over the Company's system.

The changed conditions brought about by these altered freight flows, and by the decentralization of industry, were always kept under perpetual and close review, and the difficulties created overcome by various expedients. Amongst other things, all available routes of the four group companies were regarded as one concern, and there was a constant analysis and revision of freight train movements through congested areas.

To the public generally it was work unseen and unsung. Had they known more of what was going on they would have been astonished. It was as Dominie Sampson used to say: "Pro-di-gi-ous."

How, then, was all this vast movement of passenger and freight accomplished? The answer is the old one—control—down to the most minute detail. And the main objective was to see that the greatest economy was made of locomotives, together with the punctual running, speedier working and better loading of trains and by the reduction of light running and empty haulage.

So far as possible the whole of the supervision of this gigantic business is centralized, and *Facts About British Railways* has this to say of that intricate and remarkable side of the railway's working:

> These extensive control systems are in a measure very similar to modern military organizations with communications made by extensive circuits and wireless. Signalmen, stationmasters, yard masters, inspectors, foremen and locomotive running supervisory staff, have at all times ready access to their local Control which guides their work by the wider view possessed of the movements to be made. The District Controls are, in turn, co-ordinated by the chief operating officer at Headquarters, and on the L.M.S. and L.N.E. railways, owing to their geographical layout, there are intermediate Divisional or Area Controls which co-ordinate the District Controls.
>
> In addition to the normal daily operating conferences which take place on each of the

railways in districts and divisions, and at Headquarters, a daily Central Inter-Company Operating Conference is held in order to obtain the best possible use of all available routes, and to see that they are used to their utmost capacity. The meetings of the Central Operating Conference which take place every morning, including Sundays, are made possible by a special telephone circuit which links up the Chief Operating Officer of each of the four main-line railways at his own desk. Immediate decisions are reached, involving individual or collective working. . . .

This interwoven organization of railway operating, covering all parts of the railways, makes possible far-reaching and progressive steps in the conservation of motive power, fuel and labour. . . . It enables the needs of the greatly increased services and munitions traffic to be supplied.

Close contacts are maintained between the Chief Operating Officers of the railways and the Movement and Transport Officers of the service departments, including the United States Transportation Officers, to meet hour by hour the railway requirements of the fighting forces. Movements are planned and carried through by practical and experienced railway staffs specializing in this work, with an encyclopaedic knowledge of railway ways and means.

The successful working of freight traffic in the war always called for the most careful distribution of freight wagons throughout the country, for on this depended the whole of the nation's war effort, and the responsibility fell on what is called the British Railway's Central Wagon Control. In one way or another this remarkable organization had charge of 1,250,000 freight vehicles, and its job was to ensure a good and free supply of empty wagons as and when required.

In order to avoid the running of empty trains, this pool of railway-owned wagons had been successfully worked for many years. But after the commencement of the war pooling arrangements were extended to cover special vehicles used for carrying meat and other perishable traffic, also wagon sheets and ropes. In addition, 600,000 privately owned wagons (they belonged to 4,000 owners, mostly collieries) were requisitioned by the Government on September 12th, 1939, thus completing the pool started by the railways prior to the war.

Contact was kept with the Central Wagon Control by all stationmasters and railway officials, and at certain hours every day the position was reviewed, and estimates compiled of the number of each type of wagon expected to be required next day. Indeed, every train that moved was "watched" by many pairs of eyes, seen and unseen, and the situations dealt with cover such emergency considerations as cancellations, congestions, diversions and all the hundred and one appalling complications due to air raids.

It is to this high standard of efficiency in the railway's operating departments that the astonishing flexibility of railway working is due. An efficiency that can deal with any situation under the sun. Indeed, this was one of the most responsible jobs of the many which a nation at war must undertake and fulfil.

BLITZ ON AN L.M.S. MARSHALLING YARD NEAR WILLESDEN, SEPTEMBER, 1940

CHAPTER EIGHT

THE TOOLS THAT DID THE JOB

L ET us now take a short look at the motive power, the rolling stock, the permanent way and the communications of the L.M.S. at war—the tools that did the job.

LOCOMOTIVES

In any of the Company's big locomotive depots a wide variety of passenger, freight and diesel engines may be seen—amongst them the famous "Coronations," "Royal Scots," "Garratts," 2-8-0's and the "Crabs."

Passenger engines that can pull under normal conditions a nine-coach train from London to Glasgow in six and a half hours, or freight engines that can draw 87 wagons of coal as a not unreasonable load. They are of all ages too, this representative collection of locomotives, ranging from septuagenarians to newly christened streamlined youngsters straight from the L.M.S. workshops, and costing up to £13,000 each.

To anyone with the heart of a boy—and of many a grown-up as well—there can be few more impressive sights than a close examination of so much latent power and in so small an area. Engines spruce and shining, all set and ready for the road, engines smoke-caked and shimmering with heat, just returned from a long journey, engines being coaled and watered, engines newly lit and getting up steam, engines having their smokeboxes cleared or being overhauled, cleaned, oiled, tested or repaired for yet another spell of duty.

And in them, under them, or perched above them, with oilcan, hammer or spanner, work their masters and attendants, the men responsible for the swift and sure running of these their enormous charges—the men who see to it that they are in good order for the road.

During the war, work in the locomotive sheds was no picnic, indeed most of the buildings in which the staff worked, were so blacked out as to resemble tunnels, with smoke, coal-dust, steam and darkness as their daily lot. The Chief Operating Manager is proud of the war record of these men—there are thousands of them up and down the line—and he is proud of them because they did so much and with such little fuss. "They wouldn't be here unless they were really enthusiastic," he will tell you, "It's the variety of the work that appeals—there's no monotony in the 'sheds'."

The policy of the Company after the amalgamation of the railways in 1923 had been to eliminate uneconomic and redundant types of locomotives. This was done by a programme of standardization, and gradually year by year the plan took shape.

Although this meant that on the outbreak of hostilities the L.M.S. possessed a loco-motive stock economically sound—judged by peacetime standards, it could not be expected to embrace, without a strain, the abnormal demands of a major war.

No provision having been made by the Government in more propitious times against such a national emergency, the railways, as the war progressed, were again faced with a formidable task. The obvious answer would have been to build new locomotives, but the

D

railway engine shops were soon very busy with the production of weapons and munitions, and there was an ever-growing shortage of constructional materials and of qualified labour. How all these difficulties were overcome is a story of human perseverance and mechanical strain.

Engines, for instance, were kept in traffic for longer periods between examinations. Smaller units did the job of the larger types, and obsolete ones due for scrapping were retained in service beyond their economic life. Many other rearrangements were also carried out—including the concentration of spare parts at engine sheds on a scale never before contemplated, extensive improvements in running line accommodation, the stepping up of servicing facilities, and a general inter-railway pooling of all motive power resources at contact points.

It was, in fact, a matter of every engine being worked all out, and this, of course, meant that in the workshops and elsewhere they were working longer hours too.

Other problems that had to be solved were periodic demands by Government for engines on their own account. These were extensive. They began in July, 1939, with a request for 800. It was a staggering figure, and it could not be met! As time went on, however, and with much cheese-paring, various allocations were made and as many as possible handed over. By June, 1940, the L.M.S. had been able to release an aggregate of 66, and some of these were actually used by the British Expeditionary Force—16 being lost when the enemy overran France.

There were many further allocations at different times, and these included some for overseas. In February, 1941, diesel engines were needed for service in the Middle East.

At this time, too, Germany, following her treacherous invasion of Russia, had achieved considerable penetration, and the maintenance of supplies to our new allies had become of vital importance. How could they be helped? One solution was found in the newly extended railways of Persia, which provided a link between ports on the Persian Gulf, and the southern gateway of Russia. For this work 150 powerful locomotives were required, all capable of making the heavy grades on the 6,000 feet snowcapped and mountainous stretches of the Persian railways. And they were required urgently. Soon they were on the way, and of the full complement shipped, no less than 50 were L.M.S.

But that was only part of the story, for all the engines had to be hurriedly modified to consume oil, and the repercussions in the repair shops were necessarily extensive. Those engines came to be known as "Churchill's Reply," and apart from helping the Soviets, they carried supplies to our own Tenth Army.

By 1942, however, engine stocks had been improved by various small additions, and in the following year the tide had definitely turned for the better. Indeed locomotive numbers were then at a higher level than at any period since the outbreak of war. This welcome change was brought about by a step-up in the construction of new engines in the workshops, loans from America, and by the fact that Oliver Twist had ceased to ask for more! To those who like statistics, it is interesting to note that in 1944 the engine hours in traffic exceeded those of 1938 by no less than 12 per cent.

PASSENGER COACHES

Then there were the passenger coaches. At the outbreak of the war the Company owned some 17,500 and during the period of hostilities the construction of new vehicles practically ceased.

Compared with the tens of thousands of freight wagons, this may seem quite a small number, but had they all been lined up in one continuous train, they would have extended for some 200 miles. In the first few months, 3,300 of these vehicles were not required owing to the reduction of the passenger train service, but as time went on, all were fully absorbed and worked overtime. By 1943 the position had so altered that although passenger travel had increased more than 7 per cent over the pre-war figure, there was a decrease of approximately 1,350 carriages, due, amongst other things, to destruction by enemy action and the provision of ambulance trains.

These ambulance trains were an interesting feature of the L.M.S. at war. Plans were made prior to the outbreak of hostilities, in conjunction with the War Office, for the provision by the railway companies of four for use overseas and eight for use at home.

Those for service overseas each consisted of 16 vehicles, and the home ambulance trains of nine (subsequently increased to eleven). All of the 136 coaches were provided from their existing stock, and the work of conversion and equipping carried out in the workshops of the four main-line companies. Further requisitions were made later, and of the overseas trains, nine were sent to the Continent before the collapse of France, and subsequently lost.

All home ambulance trains had quarters for a resident staff of doctors and nurses, ward cars for stretchers and suitable accommodation for sitting-up and mental cases. There was also a kitchen car for the preparation of meals and a place for the storage of medical and other equipment. Home trains normally stood at suitable stabling points up and down the country, and if required for casualties, it was arranged that such movements be made by the services departments through the Railway Executive Committee.

In September, 1942, the War Office notified the railways that a further 27 ambulance units would be needed overseas, and for this consignment the L.M.S. were responsible for more than half the number. But in addition to the above, 17 casualty evacuation trains were provided out of a total of 36 supplied by the four companies to remove air raid wounded from blitzed areas, all being controlled by the Minister of Health, and stationed adjacent to the larger cities: in the case of the Company itself—London, Birmingham, Manchester, Liverpool, Glasgow and Edinburgh.

The work done by ambulance trains in the last year of the war—that is from D-Day until the final unconditional surrender of Germany—was also extensive, no less than 361,480 sick and wounded being carried.

Beyond that the story of the L.M.S. passenger coach is comparatively uneventful, but it is interesting to record various innovations and alterations that occurred in the vehicles themselves, due to war conditions. In October, 1941, for instance, the Government directed that all first class accommodation be withdrawn from passenger trains commencing and terminating their journeys within the London Passenger Transport area. Only a few of the Company's services were affected and the direction appeared of doubtful use; indeed at times, the new situation was often farcical, and after the order was in force it was a regular occurrence for passengers to seek out the former first class compartments and fill them to overflowing, with the result that they were frequently standing in them, while other parts of the train were sparsely occupied.

Structural alterations were also made in several passenger coaches, notably the installation of an extra end berth in the single compartments of some sleepers, and the stripping and conversion of a few other coaches for use as mobile offices and mess rooms. These latter were set aside for station staffs in the event of their offices being destroyed by the enemy, and they proved invaluable. Especially was this so at Liverpool, Birmingham, and Bath, where just such disasters happened—the staff quickly finding themselves in novel quarters and sitting at a long desk, supported at intervals by nests of drawers, which ran the entire length of each coach.

The curtailment of sleeping and restaurant car facilities has already been mentioned, and a further endeavour to increase the seating acommodation in passenger trains occurred in 1941 when the arm-rests in all third class compartments of modern design were screwed back.

It was one of many austerities which the traveller had to face. His was a world which seemed to grow gradually harder, not only to sit down in, but to stand up in. It also grew much colder, especially in the winter, owing to curtailment of the time during which trains were allowed to be heated.

As Lord Royden, the chairman of the Company, remarked at the 1944 General Meeting: "Railway travel now places a considerable strain on one's physical powers of endurance, not to speak of one's powers of resistance to irritation."

One by one various conveniences had to be withdrawn. Rationing saw the end of toilet soap in carriage lavatories; cotton control of the first class antimacassars; and, owing to the pernicious activities of the scrounger who stole so many rugs, pillows and hand towels, even those creature comforts had to be withdrawn.

It is a remarkable, but indubitable fact that wars bring about a decided lowering of moral standards, and, as in 1914–18, the practice of common theft was just as much in evidence. It was unfortunate that the honest were deprived of many amenities because of the dishonest, but the railways could not be expected to bear with impunity such a colossal attrition of their stocks as actually occurred. To give some example of what was going on, it will be sufficient to state that in one year—1941—the L.M.S. alone lost no less than 400,000 hand towels!

Even more difficult to understand was the mentality of those who slashed upholstery, broke windows and destroyed carriage fittings. That it was done for pleasure seems to be the only answer. But the amount of damage was very considerable, and reached disturbing proportions.

WAGONS

Of the Company's goods wagons, the majority are ordinary standard vehicles such as the five-, four-, three-, two- or one-plank. Painted grey and often seen covered by the familiar wartime red wagon sheets, they carried, by and large, the bulk of the nation's ordinary war burden. Through the day and through the night the huge flow proceeded without respite, and always it may be taken for granted, their journeys were essential and vital.

There are, however, many other wagons in the Company's stock which are designed for special traffic. Meat and fish refrigerator vans, vans for the transport of fruit and vegetables at controlled temperatures, specially constructed and electrically heated road and rail tanks for edible oils, pipe vans, shock-absorber wagons, bogies, bo-plates, and so on. Indeed there is no type of special freight for which the right sort of transport cannot be provided, be it glass, tar, bricks, acid, salt, wheat, milk, daffodils or even beer. Nor, so far as wagons are concerned, must the demountable containers be overlooked, those useful "suitcases of commerce" that can be lifted from freight train on to road vehicles for transport to wayside villages miles from the nearest goods yard.

During the war each railway company continued to supervise its own special wagons, but where practicable they were always available to other companies—such mutual assistance being arranged through the medium of Inter-Company Control.

Naturally enough, war conditions demanded that many L.M.S. wagons be specifically designed or adapted for particular needs, such needs as the transport of heavy machinery, air-screws, large castings, boilers, steel plates, guns and tanks—some vehicles being available for loads up to 120 tons.

Various structural alterations in certain wagons were carried out during the war to cater for peculiar flows of traffic as and when they arose. In 1940, for example, when the Government decided to import an enormous reserve of very long steel and iron billets, the railway's stock of bolster wagons could not cope with the vast quantity to be handled. Twin bolster wagons were therefore improvised by linking mineral end-door wagons together—the innovation being a marked success.

When this rush subsided in 1941, another presented itself—the conveyance of lorries crated for export and packed thus to economize in shipping space. To get over the difficulty, the converted twin bolster wagons just referred to were again altered, further improvisations being made at a later date for crates of an even larger type.

Some of the aircraft imported from the States were also packed in cases of such dimensions that only a few railway-owned vehicles could carry them, and the Air Ministry agreed that a number of wagons of suitable design be built for this particular traffic and put into service, all being given the code name of "Parrot," and for convenience controlled by L.M.S.

Two more wagons of new design also call for special mention. At the beginning of the war the conveyance of tanks—especially "Cruisers" and "Valentines"—was a comparatively simple business, and they were mainly moved on wagons built for a similar purpose in the 1914–18 war. But when the "Churchill" came into being, these wagons were found to be unsatisfactory, and an answer eventually came to light in the war-flat trolley, a large number of these being acquired by the War Office and loaned to the railway companies.

So also with the advent of American-built tanks such as the "General Grant" and "General Lee." Owing to the exceptional height of their turrets the British railways had very few vehicles suitable for their conveyance, with the result that another new design— the "Warwell"—was brought into service. This wagon enabled our allies' tanks to ride only 2 ft. 6 in. from rail-level, thus allowing ample room to negotiate structures along the track without having to resort to onerous out-of-gauge restrictions.

Naturally enough, the average wagon is often in need of repair, the loading and un-loading of heavy freight making its life of uncertain length. Up to the early part of 1943 all such repairs were reasonably well maintained, but the effect of the more intensive use of these vehicles, the damage caused by less experienced staff, the blackout and the retention in service of old types of wagons which would normally be broken up, eventually began to be felt.

Everything was done to alleviate the position, including the most stringent salvaging, and one particularly interesting innovation was the employment of week-end volunteer labour at many of the wagon workshops. This scheme was eminently successful, and the total number of wagons repaired during seven actual week-ends in the autumn of 1943 amounted to no less than 8,850, the maximum number of volunteers at one particular week-end being 373! A fine effort and one that was largely responsible for restoring the number of vehicles under and awaiting repair to normal.

The construction of new wagons continued throughout the war, and in the five years

1939–43 inclusive, 18,317 were built. This factor, together with the patching-up and retaining in service of 11,589 wagons which in normal times would have been broken up as scrap, resulted in a general improvement in total stocks, which rose by over 7,000 to a grand total of 294,804.

PERMANENT WAY AND COMMUNICATIONS

Last, but by no means least of the "tools that did the job" come the permanent way and the communications of the L.M.S.

Had it not been that in 1939 the Company's 19,000 track miles were never in such good order, war transport problems in Great Britain would have been greatly accentuated. And just how good the permanent way was, and how well it stood up to the colossal burden it was called upon to carry, may be gauged from the fact that where trains at the end of 1918 were running at only 40 m.p.h. with a maximum speed of 45, in 1945 the corresponding figure—and the trains were then much heavier—was 60 m.p.h., with a maximum of 75.

The permanent way is the special charge of the civil engineer, and to maintain this and all railway structures, bridges, stations, goods depots, warehouses, engine and carriage sheds, is his main task. He will tell you that he does all the jobs on the railway that no one else will undertake, a contention which seems to be borne out by the fact that he also exterminates rats and mice, and paints the faces of station clocks!

Some of his problems both before, and at the beginning of hostilities, have already been referred to: the laying in of reserves—miles of track, switches, crossings and so on, a problem which also included the storage of these materials at suitable centres up and down the widespread L.M.S. system.

But in addition to this—and be it remembered it was over and above the constant care of the line (which always went on)—he undertook many jobs other than routine, such as installing rail facilities in connection with new munition factories or Government storage depots.

Much other important work also fell to the lot of his department, especially in carrying through schemes authorized by the Ministry of War Transport to ease wartime traffic. Two of these were of major engineering importance—the Gloucester and Cheltenham widening, and the quadrupling of the main line north of Carlisle—two outstanding feats of particular significance, the former involving the doubling of two existing lines for six miles, the excavation of several long cuttings, the extension of bridges and retaining walls, and the installation of signalboxes.

For all that, the most outstanding task of the civil engineer during the war was the way in which he so speedily restored those lines and property damaged or destroyed by the Luftwaffe. A background of what he had to contend with will be found in the next chapter.

The phrase "This is an engineer's war," was in current use during the period of hostilities, and in retrospect it can be upheld with considerable justification. Especially was this so in so far as the civil engineer was concerned, but just as much so it applies to the signal and telegraph engineer and his communications, with whom the former so often worked hand in glove.

Some account of the work of the department of signals and telegraphs has already been given, and although it is not one of the giants of the railway world, what it lacks in stature and thereby relative importance is more than compensated by the innumerable instances in which its resources have been invoked. Indeed in ratio to its size it is doubtful if any other department has been engaged more actively or fully in furtherance of the war effort.

Both before and after the outbreak of hostilities it was implicated in nearly all the large number of rail traffic schemes initiated for the various Government departments where communications immediately became a matter of primary importance.

As with the civil engineer so signals and telegraphs had their own early problems— the problems of 1937–39—protection of signalboxes, materials for emergency repairs, telephone connections with the G.P.O. circuits, and connections for new emergency administrative and control centres. But later on they were faced with shortage of materials, new works to be carried out for the Ministry of War Transport and new major works and renewals on the railway's own account.

One of their biggest jobs during the war—though not one connected directly with it— was undertaken at Crewe, where a complete change-over was made from the old semaphore signalling to the very latest power signalling installations with colour light signals directly controlled by the passage of trains. This was an undertaking of considerable magnitude, including the building of two new signalboxes—one at the North Junction, one at the South.

The North box—and they are both much the same—is a compact concrete structure with a flat roof. To the uninitiated, it seems to house the most complicated electrical apparatus it is possible for the mind of man to invent. Downstairs are the switchgear and relay apparatus rooms. Upstairs in one big room stand two lengthy frames of 200 signal levers— not the heavy mechanical levers with which most signalmen wrestle, but beautifully finished silver-plated miniatures which can be manipulated with thumb and finger.

This much the uninitiated understands—this and the little lights on a miniature line-diagram above his head, which show red to mark the passage of train after train moving over the vast network of lines which the signalbox controls. But for the rest: electrical point machines, track circuits, multi-aspect colour light signals, route indicators, ground signals and telewriters, he shakes his head in considerable bewilderment.

And in this room—a room spick and span and surprisingly quiet—are the signalmen, alert and ready for anything. Three or four unassuming and dependable men whose responsibilities seem to be constant and never ending. For the war work of these men, and thousands of others like them up and down the land, no praise will ever be too high. Often perched high and vulnerable above the lines, they saw to it that the trains went through in spite of the blitz.

And yet again, like the civil engineers, the signal and telegraph engineers faced their greatest trial during the long months of intensive enemy bombardment, the tasks they then accomplished often being phenomenal. With responsibility for nearly 250,000 telegraph poles and a wire mileage that would circle the world five times, it can be readily understood when reading the story of the Battle of the Railways which now follows, how few were the incidents, major or minor, that did not deeply concern them.

CHAPTER NINE

THE BATTLE OF THE RAILWAYS

THE first bomb came crashing down on L.M.S. property soon after Dunkirk. It was the beginning of a period in railway history which produced the most acute problems, caused the greatest amount of anxiety and demanded of all railwaymen an unexampled amount of courage, tenacity, will-power and hard work.

Some part of the Company's precautions against air raids has already been referred to, but before going on to describe the intense series of air attacks which the railways had to contend with between June, 1940, and May, 1941, it is necessary to have some sort of general picture of the staff organization set up to send out warnings and to cope with the damage both during and after an assault.

This organization, by and large, was the responsibility of the operating department. It was a vast affair. Tens of thousands of men and women in all parts of the country had their own emergency jobs to do, and extensive and many were the human channels responsible for disseminating the news and taking immediate and subsequent action. The sequence of contacts was a comprehensive one and on paper reads like a genealogical table in reverse, with signalmen, goods clerks, linesmen, porters and so on at one end and the Minister of War Transport at the other.

As the word spread like wildfire through the Company's system and far beyond, pre-arranged action was already being taken. The man on the spot did what he could, often single-handed, engineers ascertained the damage and made immediate arrangements for dealing with it, while the responsibility for the removal of unexploded bombs was the care of bomb disposal officers on the staff of the Regional Commissioners.

Repercussions were vast and far-reaching, and it was often a problem for those at Headquarters to decide which job or jobs should be tackled first. A maximum number of men in a minimum period of time was the order of the day—or more often of the night.

The life of the railway civil engineer was one long series of alarms and excursions. Gangs sometimes numbering 200 were assembled and put into action, and standby trains carried materials to the damaged areas. On one occasion out of fourteen lines into London, only one was available, and the main feature of all such repair work was the often astonishing rapidity with which the trains were again moving through the wreckage. Soon—often in a matter of a few hours—craters were refilled and topped with ashes, new lines and sleepers laid and temporary bridges erected—some of the latter, especially over water or busy street thoroughfares calling for considerable engineering skill.

Normally during a raid the staff went to their shelters, but if there was any trouble, out they came, for their sense of responsibility was high. Day by day, year in, year out, they had "nursed their length" of the permanent way and took considerable pride in its condition . . . and here was that man Hitler trying to blast it to bits!

The signal and telegraph engineer was in no better plight, telegraph and signalling wires were down, poles were smashed, colour light signals blown to smithereens and many delicate instruments out of order. Communications and the repair or replacement of those insignificant looking copper wires on which the railway depended so much—that in the main was his imperative duty—and it was an exacting one.

Every time there was an air raid warning his mind immediately flew to one or other of the Company's huge junction signalboxes, operating centres or electric power stations . . . how were they faring? . . . something must be happening somewhere . . . and there at last was the expected telephone call. Major or minor . . .? Well, he'd soon know now.

In the Barking area there were over 300 incidents on 60 miles of line, one of those incidents, a small one, is thus recorded in the Enemy Action Log Book:

> Bomb on down bank 40 yards London side of Basildon East Signal Box. All telegraph wires down. 4 spans, 24 wires. One pole broken near bottom. All glass broken signalbox. Signal wires displaced and covered debris.
>
> *Supply for Repairs.*—Cable No. 3117, 15 pair 440 yards installed temporarily.
>
> All in work at 4.30 p.m.

"We had a bellyful for months on end," said the District Signal Inspector of that part of the line. "But we got the communication through."

The situations which faced the train operating staffs were fantastic, for a railway is like a sensitive piece of machinery—machinery which consists of thousands of men, engines, wagons, coaches and road vehicles—all interwoven, and all interdependent. How passenger and freight trains were kept on the move at all, will, to the layman, always be a mystery. The problems that suddenly presented themselves, often in a matter of seconds, when a big station was heavily blitzed, were grotesque. Here men and women fought with their pencils, their telephones and their brains. Had they faltered, the country's main system of transport would have been paralysed, and the life of the nation at stake.

To all those who faced the crude and stark realities of modern aerial bombardment the strain was unremitting and intense, and be it remembered a far greater effort was needed for them to keep going—as keep going they did—without that rigid training in discipline such as the services undergo before battle.

The courage of railwaymen became proverbial. They worked until they dropped on the track and in their tracks. They were wounded, scalded, burned, and yet carried on. They flirted with death on countless occasions to save property, passengers and the lives of their own comrades. A number were killed outright at their posts. For at the back of everyone's mind was that primary duty of the railways—the service which knows no stay, no stop —to keep the lines open and the traffic moving.

It would take a large book to tell of the many recorded instances of what railwaymen accomplished when the huge defensive battle was at its height, and the following is but one of many examples to show the stuff of which they were made. It is taken from *Carry On*, the L.M.S. house magazine, for December, 1941.

> During the height of a raid, a munitions train stabled in a siding in the Liverpool district received a direct hit from a high explosive bomb.
>
> For several hours, ten Liverpool men, led by Goods Guard George Roberts, worked at the risk of their lives. Regardless of danger from continuous explosions in the munitions train and from high explosive bombs which continued to fall in the vicinity, Roberts and his mates strove to minimize the danger and restrict the damage.
>
> Goods Guard Roberts, with Goods Guard Peter Kilshaw and Shunter Evans, were the first to go into action. Wagons were ablaze from the explosion and Roberts quickly realized that unless something was done, the fire would spread. He and his colleagues started to uncouple wagons immediately in front of those that were burning.
>
> While they strove, other help was on the way. Driver Robert Bate and Fireman George Wilkinson, together with Goods Guard James Edward Rowland were on duty in a nearby

siding. Immediately they volunteered to proceed to the scene and succeeded in drawing wagons in adjacent sidings away from danger.

Driver Alexander Ritchie and Fireman William Frederick Fowler also volunteered to take a light engine to the scene and they assisted in drawing wagons on to roads away from the actual fire.

Goods Guard John Guinan assisted in the work of uncoupling wagons so that they might be drawn away to safety.

Before the first engines on the scene could get to work, the drivers had to be given the road; and here Goods Guard Kilshaw came into action again. With considerable initiative he obtained access to the yard box, which was closed, and after studying the diagram, set the road for the engine to run into the sidings.

Later, after he had returned to his depot, Kilshaw volunteered to work the fire train to the sidings and again operated the levers in the box.

For the final phase of this night's heroic story, we must go to Signalman Peter William Stringer. When the bomb fell on the munitions train, Stringer was standing at the top of the steps of his box, keeping a lookout for incendiaries.

The force of the explosion threw him down the steps and to the bottom of an embankment. Despite injury to his leg, and the severe shaking he had received, Stringer, realizing the possible danger to traffic, endeavoured to get into touch with control, but the box telephone had been rendered useless. Next he tried a public call box, outside the station, but that was dead too. Not to be beaten, Stringer set off down the road to warn the nearest N.F.S. station, but fortunately meeting an A.R.P. cyclist messenger, sent him off with the message. Next Stringer got into touch with the A.R.P. wardens, and advised them to get people in surrounding houses into shelter. He then made his way to the next signalbox and advised the signalman there to stop all traffic.

Stringer then returned to his own signalbox.

There were many other acts of bravery by members of the L.M.S. staff, several of them, as these were, being honoured by the King.

Men and women often faced catastrophic situations. They had hairbreadth escapes from falling masonry and live electric cables. They entered warehouses aflame from end to end, the girders red hot and hanging down the walls like bell ropes. They handled unexploded bombs. Women telephone operators refused to quit switchboards when their office walls lay in ruins about them. Trains were derailed and lifted bodily from the track, and drivers, firemen and guards crashed with them. Signalboxes received direct hits, huge cranes toppled over, hotel roofs fell in, horses stampeded, goods yards were gutted. The Company's fire fighting and rescue services, its ambulance squads, the railway police, its A.R.P. workers and its Home Guard worked night and day in smoke, steam and fire.

It was all a matter of ingenuity and resourcefulness, coupled with good honest British guts, and often it went on for hour after hour, and sometimes night after night as raid succeeded raid.

Indeed, no one not constantly and intimately in touch with events as known at headquarters, could possibly have the slightest idea of the immensity of the jobs that were done, and the extent of the damage caused.

The nation was being tested. If they failed there would be no D-Day.

It was the railways' darkest, and their greatest hour.

ENEMY DAMAGE TO L.M.S. PROPERTY

Berlin, Tuesday.—During the early morning bombing attacks were directed against fortresses and railway stations in England. A great number of heavy and medium bombs were dropped. Many direct hits were registered.

Material damage caused by enemy air activity was so extensive that it would be impossible in a work of this size to describe any but a few of the major scars of battle.

In brief, however, the first attack on the L.M.S. Railway took place in the Thames Haven branch on June 19th, 1940, when a bomb fell 20 feet from the fencing and caused damage to the banking and block telegraph. It was a light prelude to what was to follow. From then until August 24th raids were spasmodic and of little account, but from that date on they rapidly increased in frequency, weight and fury, became intensive during September, and reached their maximum in October, after which, although they may have been more concentrated, they gradually tapered off until the first week of May (1941) when very heavy attacks were made on the Liverpool area. Apart from a further major assault on London on the night of Saturday, May 10th, these were the last of anything like a massive character affecting the Company itself, until the enemy's last fling in the London area, when there was a heavy attack on February 19th and 20th, 1944. Up to June of that year 83 "incidents" caused damage to the Company's London property.

It is noteworthy that in the period, August 24th, 1940, to May 10th, 1941, the Company was under fire on 170 of those 260 days, and on 97 the attacks were styled as heavy.

Let us take a look in more detail at the different areas most involved.

LONDON AREA

In 1940 London suffered most. It was the main target during September and October, and traffic workings were badly disorganized on numerous occasions, with many serious line blockages. Not the least difficulty was the frequent and extended hold-ups on the routes over which traffic is normally exchanged between the four main-line companies and the Port of London Authority. This necessitated not only much extra shunting to sort out the important and priority traffic for despatch by other and sometimes much longer routes, but the utilization of siding accommodation badly needed for other purposes, to store the remaining traffic until it could be dealt with.

Many of the heavily used residential electric services, both L.M.S. and London Passenger Transport Board, in North London were also frequently interrupted by serious blockages, while the damage to railway stations in general extensively hampered traffic operations on both steam and electric systems.

At Euston for instance, on October 19th, incendiaries set fire to the roof of the Great Hall, and H.E. bombs made a crater between Nos. 2 and 3 platforms, damaging the station roof, offices in Drummond Street and the west wing of Euston Hotel, while St. Pancras was actually hit three times in a single month, on one of these occasions the station being closed for five days.

Goods stations in the London area did not escape either—eight were extensively wrecked, and many buildings burnt out by fire or utterly destroyed by H.E. Here glass roofs fell in, water mains burst, electric cables were damaged and there was loss of life.

At this time too, the Thames Estuary area (east of Bromley) suffered considerably. There were eight big raids in 1940—the worst on September 7th, when a tremendous attack developed, resulting in the main lines being heavily damaged. At West Ham an empty electric train received a direct hit, and the lines and platforms were so devastated that the station had to be closed for eleven months.

In the London Fire Blitz of December 29th, however, the L.M.S. was singularly fortunate, with the lines obstructed at one point only, and though fires were started in several buildings the prompt and efficient action of the staff prevented all except one causing extensive damage, a stable of 99 stalls being almost completely burnt out, but the horses were safely evacuated.

On May 10th St. Pancras passenger station was again hard hit, and on this occasion remained closed for a week.

BIRMINGHAM AREA

The first raids in the Birmingham, Coventry and Wolverhampton area were made on two consecutive nights, August 25th and 26th. They were fairly heavy, but attacks were intensified in October and November—when the District Control Office, the District Passenger Manager's Office, the Parcels Office and various signalboxes were badly knocked about. This, of course, meant that traffic movements were very seriously impeded, and though train services were got going again in an incredibly short space of time, other sections of the operating department frequently had to wait. At Birmingham Central, for instance, where the working goods shed and warehouse were completely destroyed, it was almost two years before buildings of a temporary character were provided.

Then came the devastating attack on Coventry, which shocked the country from end to end. The L.M.S. had its share of being "Coventrated" during this major raid, and at various points received such a hammering that it brought operations almost to a standstill. Many bombs were dropped about the stations, yards and running lines, and along with the rest of the service the signal and telegraph equipment suffered considerably.

This was the Nazis' best example of a focal attack on a limited target. Within a few hours 122 incidents had occurred on the railway itself, and what repercussions this entailed can be appreciated when it is remembered that the town lies within a triangle of lines, one side of which carries the main route from London to Birmingham and the Black Country.

At least 40 H.E. bombs were dropped on one track alone, some craters measuring up to 60 feet in diameter, and it is a remarkable feature of the repair operations that in this, the most concentrated attack the railway experienced, the main line was restored for traffic in four days and all lines in a fortnight.

No raids of note occurred during January, February and March, but there were four in April and May—April 9th, Birmingham again being the sufferer, with more main-line blockages and three goods depots isolated.

In this busy Midland area as elsewhere, signalboxes were frequently hit and damaged. An example of what this meant to the Signal and Telegraph Engineers' Department may be gathered from one of many reports—the largest signalbox at Birmingham (New Street Station), being practically destroyed by a direct hit at eight o'clock one evening.

This signalbox—76 ft. long and fitted with a 152-lever frame—had practically the whole of its lower storey brickwork demolished, and the superstructure damaged beyond repair.

Blast also destroyed about 40 levers, the instrument shelf, block instruments, telephones, batteries and relays.

The following morning arrangements were made for complete possession of the running lines and for the clearing away of 40 wagon-loads of debris. At the same time a nearby signal linesman's room was fitted up as a temporary blockpost, and provided with the necessary instruments and field telephones so that the train service could be maintained.

Two emergency signalboxes—each 43 ft. long—were then brought in by rail and fitted up, 40 new levers being added and the whole frame relocked.

After considerable alterations, rebuilding and the installation of gas lighting the points were coupled up to the levers which remained, and the signalman was back in his box eleven days after the incident.

Complete restoration was effected some days later. During the time the box was out of commission ground staff operated the points and hand-signalled trains under instructions from the temporary blockpost.

MERSEYSIDE

In this area there were six fairly heavy raids in September, one in October, and another in November. The year drew to a close with a most devastating attack on the city of Liverpool on December 20th. Damage was then caused at Lime Street and Exchange passenger stations and at Canada Dock goods station, the latter being flooded to a considerable depth owing to the bursting of the banks of the Liverpool and Leeds Canal, when there was actually too much water to put the fire out. The most serious result of this raid, however, was the injury inflicted to the arches near Exchange Station, which blocked the lines and isolated this important centre for over three months. It was a grim and testing time, for the Luftwaffe was back the next night and the next, warehouses, goods offices, loading quays being gutted, records destroyed and 130 wagons put out of action.

January and February were as a whole comparatively peaceful months, but the enemy returned on March 12th, 13th and 14th, and in considerable force, causing damage at 31 places, including 15 blockages. But worse was to come, for on consecutive nights— May 1st to 7th—there was a series of concentrated attacks mainly on Liverpool and Birkenhead, with visitations at Barrow-in-Furness and other parts of the County of Lancashire.

Here again damage and blockages were abnormal, and on all the main, branch and dock lines fell great destruction—some places being hit on several occasions. Difficulties at the docks were accentuated by prolonged interruption of the hydraulic and electric power cranes and capstans, while over and above the smashing of the stations, important marshalling depots were isolated for long periods. During that black week, movement of freight decreased by 47 per cent and it was not until May, 1942—a year later—that things were back to anything like normal.

MANCHESTER AREA

The enemy attacks on Manchester were spasmodic, with a violent onslaught on December 22nd, when the attention of enemy bombers was centred largely on the North. This was the city's first heavy raid, and there was railway damage at 33 places, the most serious at Exchange passenger station where fires took an extensive hold. Here all through-lines were blocked, and though by January 1st, 1941, one up and one down line was available for trains not stopping at the station, the station itself was not opened for passenger service until the 13th, and then only for a limited amount of traffic.

Other damage in this district included several goods stations. At Ancoats, for instance, the warehouse was wiped out; at London Road the stables were damaged, and a signalbox gutted, and at Salford telephone circuits serving the Divisional Control Office were put out of use.

Manchester was again heavily raided the next day (December 23rd), a climax being reached at 11.45 p.m., when there was a violent explosion, apparently from a cluster of H.E. bombs. This occurred in the vicinity of No. 16 platform at Victoria Station where all the buildings, both here and on Nos. 14, 15 and 17, were either totally destroyed or extensively damaged, considerable difficulty being experienced in subduing and extinguishing fires owing to the failure of the main water supply. The damage also included the total destruction of the Divisional Control Office and many of the Divisional Superintendents' Offices. If this were not enough it was then found that the Emergency Control Office, which had been provided against the loss of the Divisional Office, was flooded and the control telephone communications put out of action; a calamity necessitating the hurried rigging up of a Control Office in some nearby cellars.

This was one of the most serious incidents in the L.M.S. Battle of the Railways, for the main nerve centre of the system in this large division was temporarily knocked out.

Such extensive trouble in a so densely populated industrial and commercial area literally played havoc with the extremely heavy passenger, freight and coal traffic then on the move, conditions being made worse by the fact that the following day was Christmas Eve. Indeed the situation could scarcely have been more appalling, but by one expedient or another services were gradually on the move again, though it entailed the handling of passenger traffic and much of the freight at outlying stations two or four miles away, and by the blocking back of a large portion of the goods and coal trains.

Reactions were of course widespread, especially in Lancashire, Yorkshire and Derbyshire, and particularly serious within a 30-mile radius.

Elsewhere the tale was much the same. Sheffield had its first heavy raid on December 12th, and on January 15th, H.E. bombs fell on the passenger station at Derby, killing four passengers and two servants and injuring three passengers and five servants—the platform roof being demolished for 100 yards. In February there were no attacks of note at any point except Swansea, and by and large, this town escaped comparatively lightly, and Leeds even more so.

In March (the Clydebank blitz) and again in April and May, there were several damaging attacks in Scotland, but so far as the L.M.S. itself was concerned the Company was fortunate and only suffered severely in the neighbourhood of Greenock.

To complete this short survey, Belfast—the headquarters of the L.M.S. in Northern Ireland—cannot be overlooked. Here several smaller raids culminated in a heavy attack on May 4th, when all the passenger platform roofs more or less disappeared, and the inward and outward goods sheds were destroyed. Carriage and wagon repair and woodworking shops were also demolished, together with electrical, permanent way shops and stores. In addition, 20 passenger vehicles and 270 freight wagons received a severe battering, being extensively damaged, while the Station Hotel was burned out except for the kitchen and a few rooms at the rear.

From early May, however, as has already been told, the raids tapered off and in the seven months June to December, 1941, there were only 52 occasions on which the Company's property was damaged. Up to this point serious incidents (excluding Northern Ireland) numbered 1,716, with running lines obstructed on 651 instances for an aggregate of 136,132 hours.

During 1942 there were but 70 incidents, in 1943 only 24, and in 1944, 83, excluding flying bombs and rockets.

On June 13th, 1944, the enemy began the use of flying bombs against Southern England, including the Greater London area, and every day until August 31st except for one day, the missiles were despatched at intervals throughout the 24 hours. In all, there were 128 flying bomb incidents on the L.M.S., the worst being at Poplar, St. Pancras, and Commercial Road. The severity of the flying bomb attacks can be gauged by the time "red" warnings operated in the Central London area. From the beginning of the attacks until September 3rd, i.e., twelve weeks, "red" warnings were in operation for 646 hours, or 32 per cent of the total hours in this period.

In the early part of September, the enemy supplemented his flying bomb attacks with long-range rockets. There were 13 rocket incidents causing damage to L.M.S. property. In November the Germans claimed to have demolished Euston Station by one of these projectiles, but fortunately, this claim like many others they made, was untrue, and the Company were left to solve the problem of designing a modern station without the assistance of German science.

To sum up: the following were amongst the most serious features of the raids so far as railway working was concerned:

(a) Damage to offices—the most outstanding being the destruction of the Divisional Control at Manchester, the District Control at Birmingham and the District Offices at Birmingham, Swansea and Liverpool.

(b) Damage to telephones, particularly control and signalbox telephones, which occurred in almost every raid—a substantial percentage of the latter through the trailing cables of drifting barrage balloons.

(c) Damage to block telegraph communications between signalboxes, necessitating trains travelling in the area affected under regulations "Caution"—the number of instances during the worst period totalling 100 a week.

(d) Trains having to pass over sections of the line at a reduced speed, frequently as low as 5 m.p.h. owing to a variety of reasons—such as
(1) Damage to permanent way where the line was not completely blocked.
(2) Damage and fires on the lineside.
(3) The presence of unexploded bombs and parachute mines.

(e) Complete hold-ups when the lines were blocked sometimes for days.

The material damage to buildings was of course colossal, and the cost of making good, so far as structures and permanent way are concerned, will run into millions of pounds.

Actually between June, 1940, and December, 1944, 41 passenger stations, 54 goods stations and five motive power depots were extensively wrecked and the principal items of *movable* plant damaged or destroyed were as follows:

	Destroyed	Damaged
Locomotives	1	73
Steam, electric and other coaches	254	2,973
Wagons (railway-owned)	1,230	7,092
Motors	37	264
Motor trailers	46	99
Drays	439	557
Horses	34	75 (injured)

By way of comparison with what was going on in the last war, it is of interest to turn to an authoritative work dealing with enemy air activities on the railways during 1914–18. In *British Railways and the Great War*, the author, Mr. Edwin A. Pratt, records that the total number of raids on Great Britain numbered a mere 108. Of these, only 79 (zeppelins 49 and aeroplanes 30) could possibly have affected the systems now forming part of the L.M.S. And by reason of the limited amount of petrol which planes then carried, and in view of the comparatively small number of machines used, the attacks were always of very short duration.

By and large, the damage was mainly one of cut telegraph and telephone wires, smashed glass and broken slates. The greatest "destruction" occurred at Wednesbury in Staffordshire, where on January 31st, 1916, the permanent way, a retaining wall, a platelayer's cabin, a goods shed and a weighing machine were all *more or less damaged*.

Some reports in the Midland Railway records actually refer to damage such as "sleeper slightly split" and "two sleepers scorched." It is difficult to suppress a smile at the ordeal through which the railways then passed.

Occasionally—very occasionally—air raids provided their lighter moments, and of these the following incident seems worthy of record. For years the L.M.S. had been the custodian of a unique left luggage item. A faked show-piece, alleged to be the fossilized remains of Ossian, one of the legendary giants who built the Giant's Causeway in Northern Ireland. Eight feet tall, and weighing nearly three tons, he became, in 1876, a ward in Chancery of the old L. & N.W. Railway, following an ownership dispute between his showmen partners.

An appeal to the Courts by the Company, to secure disposal against conveyance and storage charges being dismissed, Ossian, for the next 64 years, enjoyed a singularly tranquil existence, first at Broad Street and later at Worship Street Stations in London. Naturally enough, with those storage charges mounting at the rate of £11 5s. a year, and with out-standings eventually totalling over £700, the L.M.S. whose responsibility he became after the passing of the Railways Act, often wished their unwelcome ward elsewhere.

And thus this strange state of affairs might have been continued had not Ossian, on October 14th, 1940, been blitzed and to such an extent that, like Humpty Dumpty, he could not be put together again. Fittingly enough, therefore, the bits and pieces were used to fill the crater made by the bomb that brought about his end. At his interment there were no mourners—only a railway official summing up the situation with that trite saying about an ill wind!

.   .   .   .   .

In looking back over the whole nightmarish period of the raids, the railwayman will tell you it wasn't as bad as he expected. For one of the things he anticipated and dreaded most, was the methodical and constant bombing of keypoints, such as the Sutton Weaver Viaduct between Crewe and Warrington, which would have cut the direct route from the south and west to Liverpool, and to the North of England and Scotland, and left a trail of disorganization over large areas of the British railway system as a whole.

Havoc without plan seemed to be Hitler's principal aim. Terrorize the population and the war was over—an underestimation of the British people and the British railwayman that possibly lost him the war and certainly lost him the Battle of the Railways.

L.M.S. STEAMER *DUCHESS OF HAMILTON* BRINGING TROOPS ASHORE FROM T.S.S. *QUEEN MARY* ON THE CLYDE

CHAPTER TEN

THE WORKSHOPS

THE various workshops of the L.M.S. combine to form one of the biggest engineering organizations in the world. At the chief centres, such as Crewe, Derby, Horwich, Wolverton, Earlestown and Glasgow there are really large establishments, but a further 42 subsidiary ones are spread widely over the country from Inverness in the north to London in the south.

The principal job of the "shops" is, of course, to build and keep in order the Company's locomotives and rolling stock, but in addition to this they have many other responsibilities, such as cranes, turntables, water supplies, lifts, coaling plants, generating stations, electrified lines, and all sorts of outdoor machinery.

Pre-war the workshops' staff numbered 24,772, but during the period of hostilities, those figures increased to 29,920 (excluding 4,000 O.H.M.S.). And in that huge assembly of men and women will be found many of the master craftsmen and skilled technicians who in peacetime gave to the public of these islands the fine standard of travel comfort which reached high-water mark in "The Coronation Scot" train.

To most people, and in the words of *Punch*:

> Crewe is a fantasy of travellers' brains
> Born of the night of Bradshaw and of trains.

but standing astride one of the main trunk lines that pass through that huge railway centre, lies one of the biggest of all the Company's workshop establishments. Backed by more than a century of railway engineering tradition, it extends over an area of 160 acres, and apart from producing an infinite range of railway requirements, from giant locomotives downwards, it repairs some 40 engines every week.

The exterior of Crewe workshops is one of contrasts—of the long smoke-grimed shops themselves, of vechii covered offices and dwelling houses, of tall chimneys, some 180 feet high, of a rookery where nearby nest pigeon and brown owl and of a score of shunting engines busy drawing raw materials, stores or fuel. But inside things are more uniform. A world here of concentrated industry—of overhead cranes, of glowing furnaces, of long rows of cream painted machine tools. A world smelling of metal and oil and vibrating with the noise of pneumatic riveting, the heat of a brass foundry, the stamping of huge steam hammers and the methodical purring of capstan lathes, planing, milling or key seating machines. The main erecting shops are the finest in the country, and here at one time some 60 engines may be seen in all stages of building or repair. But there are many other shops; wheel shops, tube repair shop, boiler mounting shop, machine and fitting shops.

And about those shops go the men—and since the war the women—who have made Crewe locomotives famous all over the world. The old hands—the male staff—in dark clothes and cloth cap—the women generally hatless and clad in overalls.

At the height of the nation's war effort, Crewe employed a staff of some 7,500 and it was they and others like them in the railway workshops of the country who saw to it, and in no uncertain terms, that Britain had the motive power and the rolling stock she required.

Derby, the headquarters of the organization—the Chief Mechanical and Electrical Engineer's Department—also has a hundred years of railway service to its credit and fulfils the same sort of functions as Crewe. What therefore has been said of the latter centre applies just as much here—though Derby is equally famous for its carriage and wagon works—the largest in Europe—where 350 coaches and 10,000 wagons have been built in a single year. Here, as elsewhere, the number of vehicles repaired runs annually into many thousands.

Generally speaking, the other large centres act as maintenance and constructional depots and the smaller ones as subsidiary repairers for the main assembly shops and the railway as a whole.

When the war clouds began to pile up over the Continent of Europe it was only natural that those in high places should turn a speculative eye on the Company's fifty-odd establishments. Nowadays the armouries of the fighting forces are filled and kept replenished by skilled craftsmen using a wide range of implements from precision tools to mighty hammers. And these implements the L.M.S. had, and much more besides, including a standard of modern organization and administrative ability second to none. But apart from preliminary discussions and arrangements about ambulance trains and a general questionnaire from the Committee of Imperial Defence about workshop capacity, no definite approach was made by the Government until 1937, when the Company was asked by the War Office to undertake the design of a medium tank, and in 1938 to help in manufacturing aeroplane wings.

Special facilities were, of course, soon set aside for both these projects—so far as aircraft were concerned, it was the first occasion a railway company had tackled such a job—and when the momentous Battle of Britain was being fought above the sunlit fields of Southern England in the late summer of 1940, sufficient wings for many Hawker Hurricane fighters had already been completed, and were doubtless helping to inflict on the enemy his first setback to world conquest. Other pre-war arrangements included the allocation of accommodation for reforming cartridge cases.

At the outbreak of hostilities building programmes for new locomotives and carriages were largely suspended. Yet until April, 1940, only a small number of Government orders was forthcoming, and unfortunately this led to the release of a certain number of skilled and unskilled men, who joined the services or obtained more remunerative work elsewhere. And ill could they be spared.

The experience of the railways in the last war was, however, not forgotten by the departments' executive officers, when the workshops were so denuded of their essential personnel that it ultimately became almost impossible to continue, much less to expand the building and maintaining of their locomotives and rolling stock.

Before matters got any worse therefore, and knowing the time would come when those responsible for the direction of the present war would call upon the railways for added effort to accelerate the wheels of transport, railway executive officers felt it their duty strongly to impress this view on the Government. Meetings were therefore called to consider means of utilizing to the full the men and machines in the railway workshops, and the outcome of these discussions was the formation of a committee embodying members of the Ministries of War Transport, Supply, Aircraft Production, Labour, the Admiralty and the Railway Executive Committee. Their principal object was "to agree on the type and quantity of manufacture to be undertaken in the shops and how much reserve capacity could be allocated to the various supply departments."

Meantime, the L.M.S. workshops by personal contact with various Government departments had been extending the scope of their activities on their own, and in consequence of these efforts, and with the collaboration of the committee just mentioned, the trickle of work rapidly increased until a torrent of requests for jobs of many different types poured in. The result was more than satisfactory, for up to the end of 1943, 4,705 orders had been accepted for Government work, varying from simple machinery or casting jobs to the complete assembly of tanks and aircraft.

Some measure of what this amounted to will be appreciated from the fact that over £18,000,000 was expended on the work, a figure which does not wholly reflect the true value inasmuch as it only covers the price of such materials as were supplied by the Company, and does not include the large mass of material issued free of charge by Government departments.

The history of the workshops from May, 1940, when the vast flow began, is one of constant endeavour. After the surrender of France many and diverse were Government's demands. Invasion was in the air. Rush orders were placed for searchlight projectors, bent rails for road blocks, driver's seats for tanks, wooden parts for rifles, and later, receiver and transmitter cabins for radiolocation. They even undertook the transformation of many grocer's vans and builder's lorries into Armadillos—Heath Robinson affairs consisting of a wooden box-like superstructure lined with pebbles and resistant to machine-gun fire at close range. This contraption—it could be called little else—was allocated for the protection of men employed on defence works at aerodromes, and took its name from the burrowing animal of Central and South America "possessed of a bony armour, indifferent vision and acute sense of smell and hearing."

This however, was but the start, and in the end the final tot of work done, over and above ordinary railway jobs—still very extensive—makes an imposing contribution to the national arsenal. In aircraft alone, the output eventually rose to immense figures, including between three and four thousand pairs of new wings for Hurricanes, Typhoons and Horsa gliders, not forgetting many bits and pieces, large and small, such as mainplates, flaps and wing-tips. In glider construction the carriage builders were given a special opportunity to show their skill as woodworkers, and well did they accomplish the work.

As the war progressed a considerable number of aircraft were repaired, either in whole or part, and the "shops" became familiar with such well-known craft as Hampden bombers, Lancasters, Spitfires and Whitleys.

This novel and interesting work provided many fine problems for the executives of the department, including the erection of new buildings, the setting aside of existing space for work and storage, and all the difficulties of bottlenecks, and materials in short supply.

Planes often came straight from the battlefield via R.A.F. depots, were stripped, put on to mobile trolleys and repairs speedily carried out, down to the last coat of paint and final inspection. Sometimes they were flown back to duty from adjacent airfields.

Always it was the workshop's chief aim to simplify the work as much as possible, and women latterly took a big part. But the jobs were never so simple as they appeared on paper. Periodically the design of some wing or fuselage had to be altered, or a component had to be modified, such problems entailing much pre-production planning, the readjustment of jigs, new tools, and even the purchase of additional machinery.

Apart from construction work and repairs, several contracts were undertaken with the euphonious title of "Reduce to Produce." These entailed the breaking down of badly damaged aircraft for the purpose of salvaging repairable and re-usable components, and again the value of this work may be assessed from the fact that for the 2,000 odd parts needed for repairing a bomber, 1,000 could often be obtained from broken down machines.

The story of L.M.S. tank production "A13 Cruisers," "Covenanters," "Matildas" and "Centaurs"—is much the same as that of aircraft, and hundreds of these vehicles were turned out in whole or part, together with a huge assortment of components.

The organization to deal with tank work, like that of aeroplanes, was something outside normal railway practice, and it was necessary to recruit technicians and others from men in the "shops" who had no previous experience of administration or office work. Practically every workshop large and small, contributed in one way or another, and while some of the material such as bullet-proof plates, castings, engines, gearboxes, gun-mountings and tracks were supplied as a free issue, the remainder of the raw materials and proprietary articles had to be ordered by the Company. For some vehicles 4,445 parts were produced, and spares for all ran into hundreds of thousands.

Actually the first tank was mobile in September, 1939, ten months after receipt of the first drawing, and at one time the output was three and a half armoured vehicles a week.

But the L.M.S. munition work did not end with aeroplanes and tanks. It also produced a wide miscellany of articles such as gun carriages and mountings, millions of shells and shell components, and many steel railway bridges and trestles for the use of the fighting services.

These bridges call for special comment. Under war conditions the conventional type of bridge is often an impossibility owing to it being impracticable to survey the site and allow time for provision and erection. The War Office had therefore designed a structure which from its general appearance was not unlike "Meccano," with a complete interchange of all the various parts—this making for quick assembly under arduous and dangerous conditions.

In all, many sets of bridge spans and trestles were produced. The Railway Executive Committee ordering a substantial number of the latter for their own use, and invaluable they proved for speedily shoring up damaged bridges, arches and buildings during the Battle of the Railways. Steel for this rail job alone weighed over 3,000 tons.

Then there was help for the Navy, apparatus to catapult aircraft from ships of the Merchant Service, submarine detector parts, bullet-proof shields for men manning the ·303 Hotchkiss and much work of a secret nature.

Indeed the workshops were never idle night or day—70,000 steel castings, some of several hundredweights were made at one workshop alone, and 34 drop hammers worked continuously to turn out over 4,000,000 stampings, varying in weight from half an ounce to two hundredweights—these covering practically every phase of war equipment, planes, tanks, guns, shells and fighting vehicles.

The diversity of L.M.S. production ran from high-precision jobs, such as 27,000 gun and aperture sights for American Lewis guns (they had to be correct to less than a thousandth part of an inch), to the building of over 8,000 assault boats.

But the list is almost endless. Ammunition boxes, braziers, equipment for towing aircraft targets, pole wagons for timber cartage and even special trolleys to carry treasures from the National Art Gallery to safe storage. Nor must it be forgotten that one of the Company's steel-making plants, closed in 1932, was reopened for making ingots for ship-plates—tens of thousands of tons being eventually produced.

At the end of November, 1940, and as a matter of urgency, a novel request was made—

to break down several hundred 20-ton covered goods vans of French design and pack them for shipment and reassembly in Turkey and Egypt. It was a big job and the packing alone involved the use of 740,000 feet of timber and nearly 18 miles of hoop iron!

The provision of ambulance and casualty evacuation trains has already been touched on. All that huge conversion was undertaken in the Company's workshops. But in addition to these and after the fall of France, several armoured trains were improvised and put on rail, while many vehicles of both French and Italian make originally used on the Continental ferry service were also transformed into breakdown trains for the fighting services.

It was all a very worthy and invaluable contribution to the nation's war effort, and all of it was most willingly and enthusiastically undertaken. But so whole-hearted and generous had been the response, that it soon began to have a very serious effect, especially on the Company's locomotive position—the building and repairing of engines being in point of fact the workshop's most important and vital contribution to the nation's war effort.

The cumulative result of the withdrawal of heavy freight engines for overseas (already referred to in Chapter Eight), the reduced inflow of new locomotives, and the extensive demands for maintenance and servicing the engines now being worked as never before, was throwing a heavy strain on the organization as a whole, and its effect was becoming apparent early in 1942 by the steady and alarming rise in the number of locomotives under and awaiting repair.

The position became so painfully acute that after trying every other means to overcome the difficulty it finally became imperative to seek a reduction in Government work wherever it affected either supplies, machine tools or labour for locomotive repair or construction. This was eventually recognized by Government, and the committee previously referred to as having been formed to obtain their work, began to operate, as it were in reverse.

Asking for this release was of course a matter very much against the grain of all railwaymen, but if the position had been allowed to deteriorate any longer, disaster would have fallen on the country's main transport system, and with such violent repercussions to the producing centres of supply and to the services as a whole, that D-Day might have been considerably retarded.

There was, however, one consoling feature. The help had been given at a time when the country was in a desperate situation, and when every tank or aeroplane was worth ten, or even a hundred times as much when the corner had been turned.

It will, of course, be realized that the assistance given was not without cost to the department, and the abnormal wear and tear on plant must of necessity entail the making good of extensive arrears of maintenance and constructional work in the future.

CHAPTER ELEVEN

SEAWAYS AND AIRWAYS

(1) THE L.M.S. FLEET

IN the introductory chapter a passing reference was made to the L.M.S. fleet—the Company's ships of the narrow seas which took over from the railways at various ports in England, Ireland, Scotland and Wales, the traffic that could be carried no farther on land. Pre-war the L.M.S. controlled 49 such vessels and they operated in three main areas. These were the Clyde Coast, the Irish Sea (five different cross-channel routes) and the North Sea, between Goole in Yorkshire and the Continent. Steamships, motor vessels, paddlers, turbines—they were of all shapes and sizes, age and pedigree, ranging from little 30-ton motor launches to the large and luxurious steamers of the Irish Mail service.

In addition, however, to these seagoing craft there were yet others plying on inland waters, including the Tilbury–Gravesend ferry, various excursion and pleasure steamers on the English Lakes (Windermere and Coniston), and in Scotland, on Loch Tay, Loch Awe and Loch Lomond—the latter jointly with the L.N.E.R. Had it been possible for them all to be present at a mercantile review, they would have numbered over 100 strong with a gross tonnage of well over 80,000.

The war work of the seagoing units of the L.M.S. fleet fell into two parts, both of considerable importance to the nation as a whole. On the one hand 41 of the Company's ships were requisitioned for Government service, either temporarily or for the duration of the war. On the other—with those that were left—they kept going their peacetime commitments so far as circumstances allowed, aided where necessary by an odd collection of vessels under charter.

In the latter category, perhaps the Company's most important contribution was to help keep open the country's vital life-lines with Northern Ireland—the nation's bulwark in the Battle of the Atlantic. Here the volume of traffic passing across the Irish Sea, both to and from Belfast and Larne, was always great, including as it did the huge consignments of material and equipment for the Allied forces.

So far as Eire was concerned there was also considerable traffic on the Company's routes, including a useful influx of recruits for the services and man-power for the British factories. Indeed passenger accommodation on those steamers, especially at Christmas and at other holiday times was taxed to the limit.

Through the long years of the war one may therefore picture those L.M.S. steamers in every kind of weather ploughing through the narrow seas about our coasts, constantly on the lookout for trouble from any quarter, and doing a job that was always arduous and difficult. Against a background which often held the possibility—and at times the reality— of destruction by mines of all description, attack by enemy bombers, submarines or E-boats— their masters and crews had to contend with many additional navigational and statutory restrictions—part and parcel of sea warfare as known to-day.

This, of course, meant extra time on passage—delays being particularly accentuated if the enemy had been busy mine-laying, when harbours were closed, sailings cancelled and traffic diverted to alternative routes. Other delays, often of intense annoyance to both travellers and ship's personnel, occurred through the necessary evil of exit and travel permits, to and from Ireland, these sometimes entailing a lengthy examination of documents by immigration officers at the various ports.

When war broke out, all pleasure steamers were, of course, suspended; the utility services from Goole to Denmark and to Germany having actually been discontinued towards the end of August. And in spite of the fact that ships from this port continued to sail to Holland, Belgium and France up to the time of invasion the Company was particularly fortunate in leaving no vessels behind when the enemy broke through.

A number of the Goole steamers went on trading, for a period, with the Channel Islands, carrying, amongst other things, cargoes of new potatoes, and on the evacuation of Jersey and Guernsey, the Government requisitioned them to carry the Royal Island Militia, their wives, children and others to England.

In September, 1939, services in the Clyde were considerably restricted due to Admiralty and military requirements, and where pre-war, 4,250,000 passengers were carried annually, the volume dropped, in 1940, to less than 2,000,000. But the number steadily rose again as the war progressed.

Gourock and Greenock were particularly busy when the Americans arrived on our shores, and in all, hundreds of thousands of men and women of the Allied forces passed through these ports.

Those railway-owned vessels therefore, did a great deal to meet the country's needs, and though the jobs were rarely spectacular, they counted for much, for each time a steamer reached port it could be counted a battle won. In some ways their work could be likened to that of the civilians in the factories and munition plants; the daily round being never very exciting or glamorous, though on occasions they had a chance of hitting back, and in one brush with the enemy claimed the destruction of an E-boat, and in two others enemy planes were put out of action. Unfortunately three of the vessels were lost on what was officially described as "ordinary trading," the list of casualties including some that were fatal.

In the early days of the war, the B.B.C. broadcast a talk about the "little ships" that formed part of the Channel convoys. It was given by a naval officer who obtained his material on the spot—and that particular spot was an L.M.S. coaster.

Some idea of the conditions under which the crews worked at that time (1940) will be gathered from the following extract:

As I went off in a boat to join my vessel, I thought she looked rather frail and very small. I knew we were quite likely to be in for some fun during the trip, and as we ran alongside I was frankly a little apprehensive. A few minutes later I was chatting to the skipper, the mate and the chief engineer, and from that moment I never had a single qualm throughout the rest of the trip. You just can't, when you have people like that around. They were the happiest crew I have ever come across. They were North Country men and like all merchant sailors—or all sailors so far as that goes—revelled in a real good moan. But only about the little things. About the big things—the discomforts, the long hours without sleep and the risks they were taking—they never complained once.

Most of them had sailed in that ship for many years. They had sailed through all the peace-time hazards of gale and tempest, and now the additional hazards of war were just an accepted addition to the normal voyage. They accepted them just as a civilian accepts the fact that he must black out his windows at night and carry a gas mask. Life-saving jackets were as much an everyday part of their clothing as their trousers. When they were being attacked there was never a sign of panic or nerves—never a flicker. Bombs, torpedoes and mines didn't seem to mean a thing.

One could not expect otherwise, of course, but at the same time one must remember that they had received little or no training for this sort of thing. Keeping close station in a convoy on a pitch-black night with not even a navigation light to help, is no easy matter. Neither is the art of manœuvring to avoid torpedoes, and to bring the guns to bear. All these things are part of naval training but miles from the normal routine of the Merchant Navy.

During one moment when we were being attacked the Captain turned to me and said almost apologetically: "I'm afraid you must find us rather amateurs at all this"—Well, all I can say is that if I had handled my ship half as well as he did I'd have no complaints.

.   .   .   .   .

It was, however, the other ships of the Company's fleet—the two dozen vessels requisitioned for Government service, which saw most of the fun. Let us now look at the record of a few of these, and the sometimes dramatic part they played in the Nazi war.

To holiday-makers who remember them in their colourful peacetime settings, it will be difficult to picture them as ships of war. But soon after the outbreak of hostilities many were defensively armed and dressed in Admiralty grey—their crews trained in gunnery and other arts of modern sea warfare.

Up to the end of 1943 some idea of the different duties they were called upon to undertake will be gathered from the fact that they acted as military transports, assault ships, hospital carriers, boom defence craft, armament store issuing vessels, minelayers and minesweepers. And it is particularly interesting to note that several of the latter rendered noble service in a similar capacity during 1914–18.

A careful record of their war service was kept by the L.M.S. Marine Department and the Company as a whole may well be proud of these gallant craft and their crews. For though they were on occasions either shelled, machine-gunned, bombed, torpedoed or mined, they always upheld the fine traditions of the service which had adopted them. Many assisted at the evacuation of the B.E.F. from France, and here is the story of the S.S. *Scotia* (Captain: W. H. Hughes), a one-time Irish Mail steamer of 3,454 tons.

After making one trip to Dunkirk in which 3,000 troops were landed safely at Dover— a voyage not without "incidents"—for it included a hit on the bilge keel by a dud torpedo, and spasmodic shelling from shore batteries—the *Scotia* coaled and returned to the coast of France. After being bombed on the way over she again put into the port of Dunkirk—on this occasion 2,000 French troops being embarked—and thus laden she immediately set off for England. But the *Scotia* never got there. For hardly had she left harbour than enemy bombers came swooping down to the attack in flights of four. In a hot fire from the ship's guns the first formation dropped their bombs without result, but the second was more successful; machine-gun bullets spraying like hail all round the bridge and funnels, and bombs falling abaft the engine room and on the poop deck.

Finally came the fatal blow when the third formation secured more direct bomb hits, one actually down the after-funnel and another on the vessel's stern.

In the deafening explosions that followed, the ship shuddered, lost speed, and heeling over to starboard, gradually began to sink by the stern. With her engines stopped, there was now, of course, no alternative but for Captain Hughes to give the order to abandon ship, and those boats that were undamaged by the bombs were lowered into the water. As can be imagined, conditions were appalling and chaotic—the efforts of the ship's crew being further complicated by the fact that the war-weary French troops could not understand English.

Fortunately the commander of a destroyer lying at Dunkirk had already received the

BUILDING MATILDA TANKS AT HORWICH

ship's S.O.S., and it was with considerable relief that those on board saw him coming full speed to their rescue. In due course this destroyer, with other ships in the area, had taken off a large number of troops, and others were picked up from the sea, but the final list of casualties was heavy, many being machine-gunned in the water by enemy aircraft. Needless to say the crew acquitted themselves with admirable valour, and in the final list of awards Captain Hughes—true to the traditions of the sea he was the last to leave his ship—received the D.S.C., his bo'sun and two seamen the D.S.M.

A light-hearted, but typically British postscript to the whole affair was the comment of the *Scotia's* purser. "The sinking itself," he said, "was not very spectacular. I could not swim at all, but I propose to learn to swim now."

Other L.M.S. ships also did their part in those epic days of May and June, 1940. For instance, in evacuating British and French troops from St. Valéry, the *Duke of York* (ex-Belfast–Heysham), was shelled by German coastal batteries from the cliff-tops, and sustained damage. In the course of this action one shell fell on board and failed to explode. The chief officer, Mr. B. Williams, promptly picked it up and threw it overboard—an act for which he later received a decoration.

Then there was the *Princess Maud* (ex-Larne–Stranraer); she also suffered from the attentions of enemy shore batteries. This was at Dunkirk and there were a number of fatal casualties. With temporary repairs, however, she was able to continue her job of evacuation, and on one trip from France dogs of all description scrambled on board, and along with hundreds of troops were landed at Folkestone. Later this vessel helped evacuate troops near St. Valéry by lifeboats, some remaining on the beach until two enemy tanks came rumbling down a village street leading to the shore.

But nearly every ship had some such story to tell. They saw service from Iceland to the Mediterranean. On one occasion, towing away from St. Malo a disabled Admiralty store vessel which was laden with petrol and ammunition; on another, grabbing a cargo of copper from under the noses of the enemy before leaving Bordeaux. In all, eight of these requisitioned vessels were lost, including—and a hard blow to the Company it was—the almost new *Princess Victoria*, specially built in 1939 for the Stranraer–Larne motor traffic.

Owing to the nature of their operation there is little to report on the invaluable activities—the hard daily routine—of the many Clyde paddle-steamers, nearly all of which were called up for service and converted to minesweepers. Some, however, received honourable mention in the booklet *His Majesty's Minesweepers*, prepared by the Ministry of Information for the Admiralty, and it is sad to think that three of those gallant little ships will see the River Clyde no more.

In addition to the services rendered by the foregoing ships, four of the Company's dredging craft, two tugs and three ferries were requisitioned for Government purposes during the European war. The Company also had the misfortune to lose a steam hopper barge (not on requisition) through enemy action.

Some idea of the work done on active service by the L.M.S. fleet will be gathered from the list of decorations won by members of the crews serving aboard at the time.

These were:

D.S.O.	..	..	..	1	O.B.E. and M.B.E. ..	..	7
D.S.C.	..	..	..	4	B.E.M. ..	.. ..	5
D.C.M.	..	..	..	1	Meritorious Service Certificate		1
D.S.M.	..	..	..	3	Mentioned in Despatches	..	5

F

(2) *DOCKS*

Before leaving the shipping activities of the L.M.S., a word must be said about the Company's docks and harbours and how they operated during the war. Considerations of home security had inevitably made more complex the working of all the undertakings on which the L.M.S. services were based, and especially so was this the case with Ireland. A visit to one of the ports which normally handled many thousands of holiday passengers, would have revealed it as a guarded fortress. Everywhere there was contrast to the happier days of peace. The tourist with his golf clubs, his motor-car and his caravan had suddenly been transformed into the serviceman with his weapons, his tank and his armoured trailer. It was the same too with general freight as civilian production switched from unessentials to the essentials of war.

The contrast was even more marked at night, especially at those times when, pre-war, an eager mass of humanity had surged on or off the waiting steamers. For the docks were now hushed in a semi-quiet, with little to break the silence but the distant chatter of a winch, the periodic jangle of buffers from an adjacent siding, or the footsteps of the military patrol echoing up and down the quayside.

Coastal curfew, which restricted the arrival and departure of ships to the hours of daylight was, of course, responsible for this. But the privileged visitor would have soon realized that the port was far from asleep, for shadowy figures in duffle coat or sou'wester, could frequently be seen about the decks of tied-up minesweepers, or around the base of silhouetted gun barrels pointing skywards from escort vessels.

L.M.S. docks were indeed charged with the atmosphere of war, acting, amongst other things, as vital links between the vast production centres overseas and the nation's home and battle fronts.

The great importance of working the country's docks efficiently in wartime, and the radical change in the conditions under which this might have to be done, was visualized some years prior to the outbreak of hostilities.

As has already been told, a concentrated attack, particularly on the east and south-east coasts, had been anticipated, and it was assumed that this would lead to the intensified use of every available dock and shipping facility in the west; a factor which would call for a high standard of organization, and one in which the Company would be called upon to play a leading part.

As a first step to this end, therefore, a complete survey of the working capacity of all ports was undertaken by the Government, such being related to the ability of the various forms of land transport to clear traffic from the ships. This naturally entailed particular attention being paid to getting trains away as quickly as possible from the unloading steamers, and it was as clear as daylight on whom the main rail transport would fall. Incidentally, that survey was particularly important, for it soon became evident that the maximum discharging capacity of some ports on a 24-hour basis would greatly exceed rail clearance, so where practicable all relative steps were taken to have these readjusted and improved.

Concurrently with those plans, machinery was also set up whereby on the outbreak of war all docks and harbours in the United Kingdom were to be brought directly under the control of the Minister of War Transport. To exercise such control, Port Emergency Committees were formed at each of the principal and medium ports—membership covering such kindred fields as shipping, trading, labour and transport—rail and road. L.M.S. undertakings were of course included in this arrangement, while at other than railway-owned docks a railway representative was usually a member of the committee.

Finally, all reasonably adjacent storage facilities were surveyed and earmarked for use should the need arise.

In point of fact, the power of these committees actually included everything from the berthing of a ship to the despatch of the cargo inland, with an overriding care to secure the most efficient operation of the port in whatever circumstances might arise.

Thus a complete organization was set up for handling all imports, and when it was finally linked with a Ministry of War Transport organization, controlling the port of entry of all incoming ships, a comprehensive and essentially workable scheme was ready for action.

And so, on the outbreak of war, the change-over was made and the new order came into being—continuing, in essentials, to function unchanged throughout the period of hostilities.

War naturally imposed many difficulties and handicaps on the Company's ports, and in common with other undertakings, the Company soon had to adapt itself to new demands—principally, that constantly recurring bogey—speed in the turn-round of vessels due to U-boat activity, and the need for much overtime and Sunday work.

With the expansion of industrial activity, increasing work for the services and the frequent diversion of vessels from their original ports of entry, docks often had to deal with quantities and types of traffic other than those they were accustomed to.

Pre-war, for instance, the business of one such L.M.S. port was largely concerned with the import of iron ore and similar rough cargoes for bulk discharge. But after the outbreak of war it had to be extensively reorganized to include the export of military stores and vehicles; this entailing different labour and supervision, together with many alterations to normal procedure.

Similarly, another port which handled bananas and timber, and the *export* of coal, suddenly found its activities diverted to the *import* of coal and to the accommodation of large quantities of R.E. material on extensive timber storage grounds thrown vacant under war conditions.

A third, pre-war, handled fish. This was on the west coast, and the heavy diversion of trawlers from harbours such as Hull and Grimsby in the east, soon gave rise to port working problems of great magnitude.

But it was the same nearly everywhere else. Several of the smaller ports and piers often took on jobs they would never have even contemplated pre-war, particularly when large ocean-going vessels anchored offshore and discharged their cargoes overside into coasting craft for transfer to the wharves. Other uses to which the L.M.S. ports were put included the provision of a site for Admiralty ship repairs, the accommodation of tank landing craft and the training of their crews.

As was the case with the railways, many structural alterations had to be carried out at several of the docks—such work as dredging, piling and warehouse extensions; while various new labour-saving devices, including electric travelling cranes, road mobile cranes and electric bogies were also installed.

A sufficient and competent labour force was of course always of paramount importance, and it was frequently very difficult to obtain. Various experiments to solve this problem were, however, tried out, some with marked success—in more than one instance stevedoring firms with their office staffs and dockers being transferred from one part of the country to the other.

(3) AIRWAYS

In common with other railways and in conjunction with shipping companies, the L.M.S. had been developing various air services for some time prior to the outbreak of war. These were all operated by air companies in which the Company held shares—generally speaking, in proportion to their interest in the surface routes.

Naturally enough, the air routes sponsored by the Company were over their west coast lines between London, the Midlands, Lancashire, and Scotland, and over the sea routes to Northern Ireland, the Isle of Man, the Western Isles of Scotland, the Orkneys and Shetlands.

When hostilities broke out it seemed that the valuable pioneering work of these pre-war years would be seriously interrupted for all air services were then suspended by order of the Government, and the aircraft and personnel placed at the disposal of the Air Ministry. Plans for such a transfer had been ready and pigeon-holed for some time, and on September 1st, the various organizations switched over to a war footing—either repair and maintenance jobs or actual flying work under direct control of the Ministry.

Reporting to stations in the south of England, they helped maintain speedy communication with the British Expeditionary Force—largely the transportation of staff officers and medical supplies. Some of the aircraft were actually in France the day war broke out, and before hostilities were many days old they had brought back to this country some of the first British casualties.

It was soon apparent, however, that the extensive requisitioning of shipping, especially on the routes to the Western and Northern Islands, would entail considerable inconvenience and hardship to the inhabitants of these distant outposts, and at the Ministry's request some of those peacetime routes were reopened for mail and other duties. Seafaring people almost to a man, it took some little time before these islanders' conservative outlook on "foreign" travel could be changed. There was, for instance, the case of the crofter who refused to venture aboard until he had made his will, and of the old lady who on her first flight confessed that it was small point her being a good Christian if she was afraid to die.

But gradually the islands became air-minded and on one occasion, with only two vacant seats available, 15 people tried to clamber aboard, blissfully maintaining that they didn't mind if they had to stand!

Some of the journeys from the islands were of a humanitarian character, and in air ambulance work, 700 emergency cases (accident and maternity) have been flown to hospitals in Glasgow and elsewhere, the journey taking some two hours against a sea and rail passage, which, with uncertain shipping connections, might involve delays of a day or even more.

One of the most dramatic incidents where quick transport was so invaluable, concerned six sailors who—their ship torpedoed in the Atlantic—were driven ashore after many days in an open boat. A tricky beach landing by a Scottish Airways plane was, however, successfully made, and the sailors quickly flown to the mainland for the hospital treatment so urgently required.

During the first winter of the war, flying conditions were extremely difficult, and the presence of hostile aircraft around and over the coastal areas made some routes particularly hazardous. Indeed pilots occasionally found themselves, like doves amongst the eagles, in the middle of aerial battles—a German plane on one occasion following in one of the regular service craft to the landing field at Stornoway, and shooting up the aerodrome almost before the pilot had got out of his cockpit. It was largely due to their ability, and that of the crews, that out of all the operations undertaken from the outbreak of war to the fall of France, no machines were lost—operations, be it said, that involved flights of nearly a million aircraft miles.

In the spring of 1940, Government decided that for the convenience of service personnel and others engaged in the war effort it was essential to provide arrangements for more rapid communications between a number of other points—especially sea crossings. Under an agreement with the Air Ministry therefore, the railway associated companies grouped themselves to form the Associated Airways Joint Committee, and in the next paragraph the routes worked are given, the old companies still retaining much of their individual pre-war status.

Company	Route
Railway Air Services, Ltd.	Liverpool–Belfast–Glasgow.
West Coast Air Services, Ltd. ..	Liverpool–Dublin.
Scottish Airways, Ltd.	Inverness–Orkneys–Shetlands.
Scottish Airways, Ltd.	Glasgow–Campbeltown–Islay.
Scottish Airways, Ltd.	Glasgow–Stornoway.
Scottish Airways, Ltd.	Glasgow–Tiree–Barra–Benbecula–North Uist.
Scottish Airways, Ltd.	Inter-Orkney Islands.
Isle of Man Air Services, Ltd. ..	Liverpool–Isle of Man.
Gt. Western and Southern Air Lines, Ltd.	Land's End–Scilly Isles.

Note—In all of these companies except the last, the L.M.S. had a substantial interest.

The Associated Airways Joint Committee began its work on May 5th, 1940, operations being carried on in accordance with the public and national need, though subject to various provisions by the Air Ministry.

But it was not for long, indeed before the committee had even time to settle down all services were suspended. This occurred on May 17th, a sequel to the growing momentum of the enemy's invasion of the Low Countries and France. Followed a short resumption and yet a further suspension, this time for standby purposes in connection with the evacuation of the B.E.F. at Dunkirk and elsewhere.

That standby order was effective until June 3rd, and once again operations were resumed, but services were again discontinued on the 15th, and seven aircraft ordered to France. Though four of the machines that crossed the Channel had to be abandoned at Bordeaux, all the air crews got safely back. In one case the pilot actually flew away his aircraft almost under the eyes of the enemy, but experiencing engine trouble over the Channel, had to land in Jersey. Finding another aircraft there undergoing repairs, and with the aid of his radio officer and flight engineer, he was able to exchange an engine from this machine for his own unserviceable one and thus fly safely home to England.

That aeroplane was one of the last to get away from the Channel Islands before the German occupation, and now bears this plaque as a memorial of its services:

Aircraft G AFOI
War Service in France
September 1939 to June 1940
With Scottish Airways Crews

Services were resumed generally on June 27th, 1940, and continued with various alterations and adjustments in the light of circumstances and the national need, for the rest of the war. The routes operated by the railway associated companies at the end of 1944 were as follows:

Railway Air Services, Ltd. ..	London–Liverpool.
	Liverpool–Belfast.
	Glasgow–Belfast.
Scottish Airways, Ltd.	Glasgow–Western Isles of Scotland and the Hebrides.
	Inverness–Orkneys–Shetland.
	Inverness–Stornoway.
Isle of Man Air Services, Ltd. ..	Liverpool–Isle of Man.
West Coast Air Services, Ltd. ..	Liverpool–Dublin.
Gt. Western and Southern Air Lines, Ltd.	Land's End–Scilly Isles.

In addition to these services, special flights were undertaken when required on behalf of Government departments.

During the four years following June, 1940, the companies associated with the railway companies have, in spite of restricted routes and services, operated 6,000,000 aircraft miles and conveyed no less than 250,000 passengers. They also carried 6,000,000 pounds of urgent mail and freight—regularity of service being over 95 per cent and on some routes nearly 100 per cent! All this in the face of fog, snow, frost, icing in clouds, high velocity winds, thunderstorms, and lightning, when windows have been blown in and wireless damaged. Indeed on occasions the wind has been so strong that on some of the island landing fields stationary planes have actually been turned right over, one completing a somersault.

Much of the credit for so fine a performance must go to the pilots concerned—their intimate knowledge of the difficult weather conditions met with in and around the British Isles being unsurpassed, several having over 1,000,000 flying miles to their credit.

More than once the unspectacular but efficient services of these men and their air staffs have been recognized by His Majesty the King through the Honours Lists, and their devotion to duty has greatly contributed to the maintenance of air communication in this country, under conditions never before experienced.

CHAPTER TWELVE

MISCELLANEOUS

THIS brief history of the L.M.S. at war would not be complete without referring to the activities of various other departments whose work was related, directly or indirectly, to the railway's main function of train operating. Such departments as "stores," "research," "hotels" and the wide field of business engagements for which the Chief Commercial Manager's department was responsible.

Take stores. This highly organized establishment does most of the Company's marketing, buying on the one hand 250,000 different items, from coal and sleepers to buttons and needles, selling on the other, the things it has no further use for, such as old rails, timber for firewood, condemned wagon sheeting, scrap metals and coal gas tar.

The threat of hostilities brought the stores many peculiar problems, and in 1938–39 considerable foresight was necessary in laying down stocks against that then unknown agency of destruction, the Nazi Air Force. With much attention to detail, therefore, a huge sum of money was eventually spent on bridge and permanent way materials, signals and telegraphs and locomotive spares. Further extensive disbursements were made on account of marine and the workshops—while for A.R.P. the quantity of each article ordered sometimes ran into half millions and even millions.

Great care, of course, had to be given to the safe custody and decentralization of these, and indeed of all stores, especially such highly inflammable and vulnerable materials as timber, oil, and the like. But so well was this done that only £14,900 worth was lost by enemy action. A mere flea-bite to the millions under their care.

There is very little that you will not find in the L.M.S. stores—a glance round one of many depots allocated up and down the country might reveal such diverse articles as a guard's flag, a fog signal, a wheelbarrow, a diving suit and a red carpet for the Royal Train.

In common with the housewife and her wartime shopping basket, stores gradually came to face a constant and ever-growing difficulty of obtaining supplies, practically all raw materials soon being under strict Government control, and many other items unobtainable or entailing long delays before delivery was forthcoming.

Let us take a look at some of the stuff which they handled. It is all largely a matter of facts and figures, and both are big.

The largest single item was coal and coke. In 1939 the L.M.S. consumption was 6,000,000 tons, a total which increased during the war by over 12 per cent. Keeping stocks at a safety margin was always a worry, and acute shortages often had to be faced—in some large depots only a day and a half's supply being not unknown. Every effort, was of course, made to economize and as the years wore on, even unscreened outcrop coal was used.

Reference has already been made to the production in the Company's workshops of aeroplanes, tanks and armaments. Many of the components were a "free" issue, but large quantities of new materials had to be purchased by stores to appropriate Government specifications. In 1942, for instance, goods bought on this account alone—and it was exclusive of aircraft stores—amounted to over £2,000,000, covering no less than 28,000 items, most of them quite different from normal railway requirements and specifications.

Stationery was another interesting stores issue. The annual peacetime consumption for some articles was enormous, as the following figures will show:

1,305,648 pencils.	33,000,000 envelopes.
560,880 pen points.	40,000,000 wagon labels.
6,048,950 sheets of carbon paper.	

But the L.M.S. always had a good paper appetite. In 1938 for instance, 3,200 tons were used for advertising, operating publications, stationery and sundries.

Government control of paper provided many problems. Up to the middle of 1943 no less than 60 Control Orders were issued and as a result a very close scrutiny had to be kept on all the usual pre-war paper requirements. By drastic curtailments, however, even by May, 1940, demands had actually been reduced by over 1,000 tons: roughly one-third of peacetime consumption. Examination of every single issue went on, until by various stages, 18,194 separate items had been reviewed and of these, 4,524 were permanently cancelled, 3,390 temporarily suspended, and most of the remainder reduced in size. One such item the public may remember, was thinner card tickets, an economy which meant the alteration of all ticket printing equipment.

Apart from immense salvage schemes for waste paper, the L.M.S. also set up the first stationery reclamation depot in the country, where used paper and old envelopes were dealt with at the rate of 100,000,000 items a year. Arising from this, two manufacturers were persuaded to produce envelopes and wrappers from certain of the Company's old account forms, and amongst other things, these were used to send shareholders a copy of the annual accounts. As a result, one dear old soul, finding an outstanding bill for 2s. 4d. on the other side of her wrapper, immediately forwarded the amount to the secretary, who naturally returned it with a suitable explanation!

Of the actual sales made on behalf of the Company the following will give an indication of the quantity of some items handled in a normal year.

80,000 tons steel rails.	18,000 tons firewood,
94,000 tons iron and steel scrap.	and 230,000 sleepers.

Over and above this, the stores department have for many years controlled mills for blending horse provender, shops for making and maintaining ropes and wagon sheets, and shops for the repair of watches and clocks. They even operate a factory where one-third of the clothing requirements (uniforms, etc.) are turned out every year.

Then there is the research department. Fortunately for the L.M.S., the late Lord Stamp had seen the need for such an establishment, and as long ago as 1930 had formed an advisory committee of distinguished scientists for guidance and planning. Since then research has made a gradually increasing contribution to railway development, and the other departments have come to rely more and more on its help in overcoming difficulties and meeting new problems. Now everyone is research minded, and the scientific staff forms an important and integral part of the whole vast system.

In the years before the war such successful investigations were carried out as the reduction of wear and tear on rails and tyres, train heating, water softening, fuel economy, the durability of paint, and the elimination of dirt, noise and vibration. In one way or another the result was one of economy to the Company, increased comfort for the traveller and safer transport for the trader's goods.

Above—The L.M.S. goods depot at Canada Dock, Liverpool, destroyed by enemy action

Below—St. Pancras Station, London, May 11th, 1941

Above—L.M.S. War Production: 12-inch rail-mounted howitzers leaving Derby L.M.S. Works

Below—L.M.S. War Production: women on aeroplane construction at Derby L.M.S. Works

Above—The needs of a country at war brought an immense increase of traffic to L.M.S. marshalling yards

Below—L.M.S. locomotive men in their canteen at Willesden Junction

Above—L.M.S. women porters transfer petrol cans from lorry to truck

Below—Famous Gleneagles Hotel on war service as a military hospital

It was obvious that the years following the outbreak of hostilities would provide this department with many new problems. Anyone could foresee that the war was going to be something of a scientist's affair, and a review of the staff's activities and achievements disclose how true this was. Indeed it revolved round nearly every feature of railway defence and railway economy, from the safe running of the trains down to the straightening and reconditioning of bent pins.

Problems tackled ran from chemical warfare to lighting, and from paint to motor headlamp masks. Tests were even made to determine the penetration of rifle bullets and shell fragments on railway defences and property, while during the invasion scare, experiments were carried out to find a means of anchoring "sticky" bombs on enemy tanks, and on an emulsifying agent for rendering useless petrol supplies at wayside filling stations.

Various problems arising from shortages of materials were also solved. New fibres had to be found for the manufacture of wagon sheets, and substitutes for pigments in paint manufacture. Then too, after the fall of Malaya, tin and rubber offered another wide field for exploration, and considerable progress was made with alternatives. Lubricating oil was another puzzling question; substitutes having to be evolved and tried in case normal supplies failed and animal and vegetable oils had to be diverted to maintain the margarine ration!

The department was also able to act in an advisory capacity on the many problems which were put forward by the huge L.M.S. salvage organizations—and peculiar some of them were, such as the conversion of old gin bottles into tumblers!

The chief chemist on the research staff had to give constant advice on the precautions necessary in transporting unusual and often dangerous traffic. His staff also were in constant demand in the fight against insect pests, and in the supervision of the many drinking water supplies all over the system.

Co-operation with everyone was the keynote of all the work that went on from one end of the department to the other—even going so far as to cover many investigations for Government—largely special work on tanks, gun axles, gun barrels, aircraft searchlights and special paints. Another big job—this time for the Petroleum Warfare Department—took the form of full-scale trials to disperse fog on aerodrome runways—the Company being one of many groups co-operating in F.I.D.O., the research department making the necessary photographic and meteorological records.

As the war progressed and victory came in sight, greater attention was paid to the Company's own problems, and particularly those to be met in the post-war world— the work covering such widely different subjects as locomotive frames, the best depth of ballast for the permanent way and unit construction for the building of smaller railway stations.

. . . . .

So to hotels. For luxury and comfort the pre-war reputation of the L.M.S. hotels stood high, and the establishments they controlled—in all there were 25 of them—made the Company owners of the largest hotel business in Europe. In common, however, with other hotels and caterers, they soon had to face up to the manifold difficulties which war imposed—conditions, generally speaking, very far removed from luxury, and often a long way from comfort.

The first important event in their war history occurred in the early days of hostilities, when the following six establishments were requisitioned—the world-famous Gleneagles Hotel in Perthshire, Turnberry in Ayrshire, Dornoch in Sutherlandshire, the Highland at Strathpeffer, the Midland at Morecambe, and the Welcombe at Stratford-on-Avon. Needless to say it left a large gap in the accommodation available, and ill could it be spared, for in addition various rooms in other hotels were also requisitioned—notably in Glasgow, and the Kyle of Lochalsh.

Gradually, however, the hotel services settled down to the new order, but always the main difficulty was staff—the loss of hundreds of invaluable servants to the services and elsewhere occurring in inverse ratio to the rapidly increasing demands for accommodation by the forces and the travelling public.

In the early stages this staff problem was to some extent adjusted by transfer of personnel from the hotels that had been requisitioned, but with the compulsory recruitment of women —a factor which had never to be reckoned with in the last war—this temporary relief gradually disappeared and depletions reached alarming proportions.

Thus, with all the Company's hotels working to full capacity, personnel had to be made up, however inadequately; and the way in which it was done is known only to the hard-worked and worried hotel managers, who with no priority call on labour had to fish in the open market for anything they could catch.

To these difficulties were soon added those of rationing and food control. Regulations flowed in one after the other, and so rapidly were they introduced that the provision of sufficiently substantial food for the greatly increased number of patrons became a task of considerable magnitude; things being made even more difficult by the fact that most catering could only be accomplished on a day-to-day basis. And what that meant, every housewife will remember—but with L.M.S. hotels the family was not a small one, sometimes numbering over 350 residents in one hotel, with many hundreds more coming for casual meals.

Improvisation finally became the wartime maxim and a long way it eventually took them from the days when only the best would do.

For a time some relief to the food situation was provided by the train dining-car service, but with the gradual reduction and ultimate withdrawal of the cars, travellers were soon forced to depend more and more on hotels and to an even greater extent on the railway refreshment rooms.

Some idea of the strain imposed will be gathered from the enormous increase in visitors which occurred, in those 14 hotels where accommodation—all or part—was not requisitioned, numbers actually rising from 330,000 in 1938 to 580,000 in 1943—an increase of 250,000.

Like the railway itself, L.M.S. hotels suffered considerable damage at the hands of the Luftwaffe. It was serious at Euston, at the Midland in Manchester and Belfast, at the Adelphi and the Exchange in Liverpool, and at the Queen's Hotel in Birmingham, while others did not come through unscathed. Never, however, did any hotel cease business entirely even when parts of the buildings—often considerable—were put out of action for days, in some cases, altogether.

In this connection, mention must be made of the magnificent work done by the old members of the staff—those who through age or physical disabilities had not been called up, and were able to stay on. All too few remained and the Company owes much to them, not only for their devotion to duty in those trying times of aerial bombardment, but to their efforts at all times in training the inexperienced newcomers in the old traditions and standards.

During the blitz, hotel staffs—even when some of them were wounded—attended to their guests and shepherded them to the shelters night after night, keeping everyone cheerful and supplying them with what creature comforts they could lay their hands on. They even converted a turkish bath and squash courts to provide additional accommodation—the former being used as a crèche, where on one occasion they found themselves looking after two little Japanese children dressed in kilts.

At the Midland in Manchester the roof received literally showers of incendiaries, many of which lodged in the most inaccessible places, but all were extinguished by the staff, many by the resident manager himself. At the same hotel they also had to contend with the manifold problems following the disappearance of 2,000 panes of glass from the windows overnight.

The Adelphi at Liverpool also suffered. Here the most extensive destruction was caused by a landmine, and though there were few fatal casualties, only exceptional efforts enabled business to be continued at all. But business was continued, for with the breakfast room no more, 250 full meals were actually served in the restaurant the following morning.

And never was there a case of staff jitters. Rather was the whole tense period a time of considerable irritation that work was so constantly being interrupted. As one old servant put it (a chamber-maid with 52 years' service in the Company): "What wouldn't I do to that Hitler?" and shaking her broom aloft: "Me with all my bedrooms still to do!"

Other L.M.S. hotels were blitzed and carried on in a similar way. Euston, as has already been told, was actually the victim of a direct hit. This demolished a corner of the west wing, leaving the stair carpet dangling down from the third storey like a piece of tape—a large fragment of the bomb penetrating to a ground floor room used as a dormitory by several of the female staff, but fortunately, on this occasion, they had not retired to bed. On another occasion an incendiary actually burned its way from the roof to the third floor before the united efforts of the staff extinguished the flames. And that—with every fire engine in London engaged elsewhere—was anxious work!

. . . . .

"Hotels" are also responsible for the Company's refreshment rooms. In one way or another there are 227 such, and to these may be added 19 of the useful and convenient rail-bars which made their first appearance as an L.M.S. innovation at Euston Station in 1943.

During the first two years of the war they were called upon to undertake the provision of meals to groups of servicemen and women travelling *on duty*, but though the Company struggled hard against gradually overwhelming odds, demands under this heading eventually became so great that an impossible position arose. So much so that the Navy, Army and Air Force were appealed to, and in the fullest understanding other arrangements were made. There was no alternative, for railway premises were nearly always inadequate, the staff problem always acute, but worst of all, the restrictions governing the supply and variety of food made it quite impossible to provide meals up to the standard insisted on for troops. Even so, the requirements of men and women in uniform travelling independently, either on leave, or to take up duties, soon became so extensive that it was a frequent experience for refreshment rooms to be entirely monopolized by the services. To ease this position the Company not only gave facilities for the establishment of canteens at all stations of importance, but also surrendered refreshment rooms where they had more than one, these being converted into a forces canteen, operated by the Y.M.C.A. or other voluntary organization.

Business in the refreshment rooms was rarely normal, at least, by peacetime standards. At three main-line establishments for instance (Rugby, St. Pancras, and Euston), the number of transactions dealt with *per unit* of serving staff, rose from 600 per week in pre-war years to 2,300 in 1943; the latter representing nearly one transaction per minute per unit of staff. When it is appreciated that this includes full service with cash taken and change given, it was no mean achievement.

Like hotels, some refreshment rooms suffered by air attack, and at Manchester Exchange Station, Barrow-in-Furness, and Kensington, they were obliterated, though fortunately without fatal casualties. Many other station establishments suffered damage of some sort and the staff often had disturbing experiences.

During 1943 when business was still rising in crescendo, the shortage of food in refreshment rooms became so serious that representations had to be made to the Ministry of Food, and following several discussions, arrangements were finally concluded for an increase in the supply of meat pies, cake and similar foodstuffs—items that could be easily handled and did not require preparation. This led to an immediate benefit to the travelling public, and by the same token some relief to the problem of staff—both domestic and kitchen.

By and large, therefore, it will be seen that the Company's Hotel Services did their best in the face of great and continuing difficulties. Always, however, where humanly possible, they provided some sort of haven of rest—even if it was a rug under the billiard table. The number of travellers who were served with food ran into millions, and estimated figures for refreshment rooms alone during 1944 show that nearly 60,000,000 persons were served with breakfast, luncheon, tea, dinner, light snacks or cups of tea and coffee. In addition, of course, many more were served with other forms of refreshment.

The public, in the light of their own domestic experience, were, on the whole, indulgent to the many unavoidable shortcomings both in service and the variety of food supplied. And so far as "Hotels" were concerned their attitude may be summed up in the words of Samuel Garth, that eminent physician and fair poet of the late seventeenth and early eighteenth centuries:

> Hard was their lodging, homely was their food
> For all their luxury was doing good.

There are several other departments which have made important contributions, over and above routine, to the L.M.S. war effort. Estates, with their enormous property to look after, ranging as it does from dwelling-houses, shops, farms and hotels, to railway allotments, small-holdings and even golf courses. Finance, too, had many additional jobs to do, including the compilation of accounts for the workshops in respect of tanks, aeroplanes and so on, the construction of Government-sidings, and the conveyance of millions of service men and women. This department also had to initiate and control the Company's vast collections under the new Pay-As-You-Earn Income Tax Scheme and in the first year forwarded to the Inland Revenue some £8,250,000. Many further difficulties had to be faced by Finance owing to the fact that practically no experts of military age could be retained; the Railway Control Agreement bringing in its train many serious problems and responsibilities with the result that financial controls had frequently to be improvised in view of the wartime calibre of the station accounts staff. A staff which in peacetime was some 50 per cent female was drastically curtailed, and was reconstituted with a considerably greater percentage of women clerks, thereby placing added strain upon the remaining male personnel. Work on the Company's canals also increased during the war.

Last but by no means least, there was that large department controlled by the Chief Commercial Manager and his staff of over 20,000. Pre-war, they had the job of "selling the L.M.S." Theirs was the channel through which custom was attracted, and where liaison was maintained between the public and the railway itself. Extra passenger trains for the Lancashire and Yorkshire cricket match or extra freight trains for a heavy shipment of the season's Australian and New Zealand wool clip, it was their job to get the business and to keep in touch with the operating department and see that transport was on tap.

In addition to this, however, their activities covered rates and charges, pilferage and claims, the issue of time-tables and tickets, advertising, warehousing and a hundred and one other jobs too numerous to mention. The impact of war on the commercial department radically changed many of its peacetime activities. Suddenly, its whole policy became one of conserving transport and not selling it, of co-ordinating and reducing the requirements of industry instead of encouraging them—in short, anything to keep business away—business other than the nation's needs demanded. And it was done wholeheartedly and without reserve. Judged by pre-war standards the new order was in some ways one of commercial suicide, equivalent to a manufacturer insisting by every means in his power that the public should not buy his goods.

So the solicitation of traffic was abandoned, and many of the Company's normal trading channels were partially replaced by the vast flow of traffic that emanated from the huge purchasing organization set up by the service and supply departments. But apart from this, and throughout the war, a day and night contact was maintained with various other sections of these and other Government departments on such jobs as the transport of factory workers, the handling and distribution of troops and munitions, and in the provision of private siding facilities and storage acommodation in warehouses and elsewhere.

As has been seen, once the "phoney war" ended, all transport services were put to a severe test. The department's vast knowledge of trading conditions and of peacetime distribution became, therefore, more and more valuable as the war progressed.

The change in both type and volume of travel, the arrangements for additional trains and new stations to serve war factories produced problems altogether different from normal. Conditions which were often aggravated by the partial or complete insufficiency of equipment or the inability to obtain supplies. Many were the enigmas they had to tackle in matters of road-rail contacts, demurrage, the charging and documentation of Government traffic—indeed, there was some sort of radical upheaval in nearly every normal feature of railway commercial practice.

Take the vast repercussions following the destruction of a warehouse. Many were the knots that had to be unravelled in one way or another, for apart from the countless problems that arose over the loss of hundreds of tons of goods in bulk or thousands of packages, it was their job to find alternative accommodation—a disused public house being acquired on one occasion, on another a church hall!

Contributing factors were the employment of inexperienced staff, lack of material for packing and the difficulties of working under blackout conditions, but most of all it was the black market and the receivers of stolen goods that were responsible—pilferage and theft by individuals and organized gangs reaching colossal proportions.

Every sort of preventive measure was taken to combat these underground activities, vans and premises were locked, advertising matter was deleted from traders' packages, searchers appointed, and propaganda used to improve labelling.

It was all something of a war within a war, and though the railway police were particularly active—in 1944 prosecutions numbered 3,600—the battle went on.

It is astonishing that soon after the commencement of the almost continuous air attacks on London, the sounding of the siren became a signal for thieves to take advantage of the complete blackout and the absence of staff in the shelters, to enter the stations on their nefarious work. A number of these men were arrested while bombs were actually falling and anti-aircraft defences were pounding away at the enemy.

Another of the department's responsibilities was lost property. With all the other things the traveller had to think of during the war, it was perhaps only natural that he became no less forgetful of his personal belongings. Every conceivable article was found in carriage compartments between 1939 and 1945; the Company restoring to the service departments 34,000 items including gas masks, helmets, haversacks and even rifles.

But the jobs Commerce tackled were never-ending, at the docks, on the ships, in the ticket offices, in the goods sheds, with motors, canal barges and wagons, and in hundreds of offices up and down the line, the work went on. Further afield they kept a small skeleton staff in America to maintain friendly contact with the U.S.A. tourist organizations and shipping companies, and here much useful work was done for the British War Relief Society and the British American Ambulance Corps. The exhibition of the "Coronation Scot" at the World's Fair in 1939-40 was another of their cares.

Much additional work was also undertaken on account of trading with the enemy legislation. This covered many phases such as outstanding accounts with traders, settlements with continental railways, overseas rents and property, unrepatriated British and foreign rolling stock, the exercise of lien on enemy goods—even refunds on tickets purchased pre-war in enemy and enemy-occupied countries.

One particularly interesting feature of the commercial department's work was advertising. It goes without saying that in the years prior to the war, the Company had many attractive and unique travel facilities to offer the public, and like any other commercial undertaking in similar circumstances, they used every available means of publicity to push their "wares."

Service and speed both for business or pleasure was the general keynote, and so far as the latter was concerned a glance at the map will show that the L.M.S. covers some of the finest holiday resorts in Great Britain and Ireland: the Highlands and Western Isles of Scotland, the Trossachs, the Glens of Antrim, the Lancashire coast, North and Central Wales, the Lakes, the Peak District and the Isle of Man—all these have provided countless subjects for L.M.S. posters, and many of the country's leading artists have been commissioned to paint them.

War naturally enough put a stop to this particular and individual form of publicity, and when the Company came under Government control on September 1st, 1939, it combined with the other main-line railways and the London Passenger Transport Board to carry out a programme of advertising on vastly different lines—largely to interpret closely and concisely various directions and instructions of the Minister of War Transport.

If it were possible to reproduce in chronological order the many posters and notices that appeared on the sometimes shattered walls and broken railings of the Company's property, they would provide sufficient material to make an interesting little war history of rail transport all their own.

Here could be seen by one reflection or another, the grim and stark realities of the railway's burden in all its varying tones of shade and darkness. The cancellation of the summer holiday traffic in 1939, the evacuation, the blackout, and that strange period of "normal abnormality" prior to Dunkirk, when some of the early restrictions were removed or lessened. Thereafter might be found a hint of invasion and many painfully obvious announcements connected with aerial bombardment. Those were the long and weary years, with poster and propaganda playing their part, from appeals for war savings to requests to take food on long journeys, and from the various safety codes to entreaties to salvage anything and everything for the common cause.

The volume of passenger travel throughout the war occasioned much concern owing to the increasingly heavy demands on rail transport, and advertising played a prominent part in the national efforts to curb it. The familiar phrase "Is your journey really necessary?" appeared as a plain poster and as a cartoon in a wide range of publications. It was heard on the music halls, on the radio and even appeared chalked up on walls in Libyan villages during the victorious advance of the Eighth Army.

Publicity also covered the Press, and a full use was made of films and photographs, much being done to show the actual work that the railways were engaged on, and the difficulties which the staff, including the back-room boys, had to face.

Posters on these lines were actually distributed in America—where they made a sharp contrast to the usual scenes of historic or literary associations, one of the normal L.M.S. advertising mediums of pre-war holiday tours.

CHAPTER THIRTEEN

D-DAY

So we come to D-Day, the railwayman's greatest transport achievement of the war. Seen but dimly through the long summer of 1940 and the even longer winter of aerial destruction that followed, D-Day gradually became the railwayman's main war objective. It was his grand climax to the toil and anxiety of "the years between," years which had made him—and he would be the first to recognize the fact—ever fitter and fitter to accomplish this his major task of all; the redemption of the nation's pledge, first made on the Dunkirk beaches—to return across the Channel.

Some indication has already been given of what the railways accomplished prior to the massed Allied invasion of the Normandy coast. Much had been expected of them and they had responded in full measure. Indeed, shortly before D-Day, Field-Marshal Montgomery had honoured 400 railwaymen—representative of nearly every section of rail transport—by addressing them in the shareholders' meeting room at Euston. Here he had paid a very handsome tribute to this side of their work, at the same time expressing his confidence in the support that they would give him in the tasks that lay ahead. Needless to say the Field-Marshal was immediately assured in no uncertain terms of the railways' continued and wholehearted co-operation, but what that assurance amounted to—and it was fully carried out—can best be gathered from the numbers of special Government trains run on the L.M.S. system alone. In point of fact, from under 15,000 in 1940 to 39,000 in 1943, they actually rose to the colossal total of 58,000 in the great year of D-Day, 1944! And surely nothing will ever prove more clearly than that latter figure that an efficient rail transport system is as necessary to military operations in war as it is to the life of the country in peace.

Nor must it be forgotten that with all the immense extra rail work that D-Day entailed, civilian transport was always kept going somehow, nor was there any diminution of service traffic in other directions. Convoys with reinforcements of U.S.A. troops continued to arrive, and there were the usual despatches of personnel and stores to other theatres of war in the Middle and Far East—despatches which were actually stepped up towards the end of the year. Moreover—there was still considerable redistribution of units within the country, while on and after D-Day large numbers of wounded, and thousands of prisoners of war were coming back from the coast of France—some of the latter being carried by the L.M.S. to the far north of Scotland.

One further point which must not be overlooked—the temporary withdrawal of coastwise shipping to take part in the great cross-Channel landing also meant that part of their usual burden was deflected—though only for a time—to the ever-willing horse.

The invasion of Europe was undoubtedly one of the most important events of the whole war—if not the most important—and the railways were one of the main arteries along which the means of attack would flow.

Experience of rail transport for the Expeditionary Force to North Africa in October, 1942, had already made it clear that huge quantities of stores, equipment and supplies would be needed, and—following a landing rehearsal on the south coast of Wales in the summer of

HAMPDEN BOMBERS BEING REPAIRED AT DERBY

1943—invaluable experience was gained of the manner in which ships would have to be loaded. This enabled the War Office to make an estimate of their requirements for the invasion proper, and all relative information was eventually passed on to the railways; information which included the tonnage and type of traffic to be moved, the depots from which it was to be drawn and the ports to be worked.

Under strictest secrecy the senior officials of the four main-line companies thereupon began to formulate their plans—and vast and comprehensive they had to be. Indeed the responsibility of those few men was great, for nothing could be left to chance—major problems ranging from an exhaustive examination of the full capacity of all routes to the restriction of ordinary passenger and freight traffic, and from the concentration of locomotives and trained men at key points, to such other vitally important matters as the supply of wagons, additions to tele-communications, and the drafting of extra staff. Through long months of planning it was their constant endeavour to ensure that no possible hitch or breakdown could occur to the huge flow which the service commanders required—and required to be maintained. Nor did they overlook the importance of making sure that every movement, probable or improbable, should be as flexible as possible with a full provision against every conceivable emergency that might arise.

In due course, therefore, all those carefully made plans were completed and held in readiness and when the call came, the success of their painstaking work was immediately apparent.

Although D-Day proper was June 6th, 1944—D-Day for the railways was considerably earlier. Actually the movement of personnel into position had been proceeding unobtrusively during the winter of 1943-44, but the official date for the beginning of the large-scale concentration of troops was March 26th. And it was on that particular day the Operating Manager of the L.M.S. lifted his telephone and heard that the railway's greatest test had come and that the tense days of waiting were over.

From then on, practically the whole of the south of England became a huge concentration area—the process of building up the Allied forces necessitating large contingents being transported from as far afield as the Highlands.

Down the country's well-known lanes of travel they came, those fighting men of the greatest army that had ever left this country on such a huge and united sea-borne expedition—men of the homelands and all the Dominions and Colonies, men of America and representatives of many of the occupied countries of Europe. It was like some huge spring migration of the birds—but whereas the birds were then going north to build their nests, this particular migration was going south to destroy the Nazi nests of massive concrete fortifications on the other side of the Channel. Naturally a proportion travelled by road in their own transport, but nearly all tanks and tracked vehicles were conveyed by rail because of the distances involved.

On the L.M.S. the largest group of trains was worked from Scotland to destinations on the Southern Railway—the majority moving over the Company's system for distances exceeding 500 miles, with tanks, in particular, causing a considerable strain on line capacity owing to the necessity for working these bulky and heavy loads at comparatively slow speeds.

And here it is but fitting to record the close and friendly collaboration which existed during those historic days between the main-line railway companies and the service departments, for extraordinary demands were often made by the latter and nearly always were

G

they fulfilled to the last letter—the services on their part being ever ready to give sympathetic consideration to any difficulties encountered, and a way out generally found to the satisfaction of everyone.

All rail records in that great concentration of Allied might went by the board. Including D-Day traffic and other military requirements covering the period of 11 weeks—March 26th and June 24th—the L.M.S. ran no fewer than 13,729 trains—the highest weekly total being 1,585—a figure which takes no account of the thousands of wagons sent by ordinary freight trains. Furthermore, once the beach-head was firmly established there followed a sustaining flow, which gradually increased in volume to maintain the invading forces. As the pace quickened, additional ports to those selected for the initial assault were brought into the scheme until nearly every such undertaking in Great Britain handled invasion traffic.

It was all a matter of teamwork between railway, military and dock authorities, for never a ship was delayed or a special that did not run to programme. Every member of the operating staff was in on the job, and all of them—from those stationed far away in the Company's distant outposts, to those on liaison and other duties within sight of the vast sea armada, on the Southern Railway—worked as never before.

So well was the secret kept that until the official news broke a few hours after the troops had landed on the Continent, only a very small proportion of the Company's staff knew exactly what was afoot. But many must have guessed, and fervently prayed that this was the beginning of the real thing at last.

Those indeed were days of great and successful endeavour, and the L.M.S. Operating Department may well look back with satisfaction on their contribution to the common cause. The words of one of the Company's divisional superintendents were expressive of much that was going on over the huge network of lines—"Nothing," he said, "has given me a greater thrill anywhere or at any time, either in my private or railway life, than the way my lads have risen to this great occasion."

So far as traffic was concerned, the flow of trains never stopped and the problem was often to get the proverbial quart into the pint pot. At one key point, for instance, as many as 150 extra special trains were passing through in a day. . . . But—"We were nicely busy," was the most the District Controller would admit to—and what a perfect example of proverbial British understatement that was. It was, however, typical of hundreds of others up and down the line—the modest assessment of what the Company was doing and did.

Sometimes a wagon broke down, but plans were so well organized that a quick call to the War Office with full details of the contents, soon resulted in instructions being given for another wagon with similar materials being immediately sent forward. In this way ships loading in the ports never failed to receive their scheduled cargo complete.

"Meet an L.M.S. stationmaster," says *Carry On*, the Company's house magazine.

"Six times my usual number of staff, still up to the neck and we've all thoroughly enjoyed it."
Every day from his station were despatched compo packs, canned fish, canned milk, ship's engines, pontoons, ambulance stores, army motor bicycles, telegraph poles and gun turrets.
But not all stations had to deal with such a variety of war traffic, others concentrated on single consignments only. One station, for example, sent tons and tons of steel mesh for use on the invasion beaches, another, thousands of miles of barbed wire or thousands of army blankets, elsewhere it was camouflage netting or 30-ton cranes—even mountains of kitbags (invasion troops' personal property being returned to their homes), or rails and sleepers for the railway battalions which were soon following the spearhead of the attack.

On the coast a small seaside station was particularly busy with jeeps, and on one day —a day or two before D-Day—four porters beat their own record, getting away 50 wagon-loads. But the list of stations and the materials they handled was almost endless. The huge system of the Company was throbbing with the biggest freight flow of its history and it was moving on oiled wheels in more senses than one.

The trains were endless, too, and while the peak period was around D-Day, the flow went on until VE-Day and beyond. To show the part played in the post-invasion period, i.e., D-Day to December 31st, 1944—the War Office have stated that 14,763 special *invasion* trains were run on British railways. During the same time the number of trains run by the Company have been calculated, and they amount to 7,291; so that it may be claimed nearly 50 per cent of the total number of trains worked in that vitally important period travelled L.M.S. for at least part of their journey.

But few people will ever have any real conception of the work that was done—clearing the marshalling yards of empty wagons was a major job in itself. Train crews were never idle, motor vehicles and the Company's carts worked overtime, the backroom boys on the operating staff, clerks, telephonists, typists, were on their toes as never before, the civil engineer and his opposite number in the signals and telegraphs standing by ready for any and all emergencies.

As the Allied advance progressed, the use of ports further up the French and Belgian coast, and the changing shipping situation caused many amendments to the scheduled programme of rail transport. On such occasions whole blocks of trains were frequently postponed, sometimes for as much as a day or so, and often specials had to be stabled en route until ships were available and the docks could deal with them. Far back along the L.M.S. system the repercussions of these hold-ups were felt and to meet them necessitated the strictest vigilance both day and night.

Sometimes the War Office asked for special trains to be worked through in a particular hurry—an example of one such priority consignment came to the Company in an urgent call for rubber boots for the Allied forces when they advanced into Holland. Part of this order—17 wagons—was immediately loaded up at Stirling in Scotland and run through post-haste, stopping only at Leeds to take on a further 15 wagons. Everywhere on its long journey south that special was speedily nursed through under the watchful eye and care of hundreds of L.M.S. operation experts, and it arrived in time—to be loaded aboard a steamer bound post haste for Antwerp.

Some idea of the really heavy traffic sent overseas to the Continent at this time is illustrated in the following selected list:

Ambulance trains.	Tanks and other fighting vehicles.
Steam and diesel locomotives.	Motor-cars and lorries.
Railway wagons (often full of coal).	Guns and ammunition.
Breakdown cranes.	Bridging material and pontoons.
Mobile workshops.	Fuel.
Oil and petrol.	Foodstuffs for liberated nations.
Sledges and folding boats.	

But though most of the honour and glory must go to the Operating Department for the full triumphs of the Company's part in D-Day, they would be the first to pay tribute to the support they received from the other departments of the Company, and of these there is the Fleet's part in this historic and momentous feat of arms. Not so spectacular as Dunkirk, but for all that they did yeoman service in forming part of the bridge of boats to the Normandy beaches.

For instance, the *Duke of Argyll* anchored off Courselles at 6.5 a.m. on D-Day, and successfully discharged her assault troops, the Second Battalion Canadian Scottish Rifles, next day being back in England to embark U.S. troops for Utah Beach in the American sector.

The *Duke of Lancaster*, refitted as a hospital carrier, also had her assignment—to arrive off the French coast on D-Day-plus-2, her water ambulance boats eventually running a steady service to the beaches with seamen, firemen and stewards all lending a hand in the work of unloading and carrying wounded aboard en route for home. Journeys similar to this soon became a regular feature of this vessel's service, and it was her proud record, together with several other such carriers, that the beach-heads were never without their familiar white hulls and red crosses. Later, in the autumn, the *Lancaster* operated from the recaptured ports of Ostend, Dieppe and Cherbourg.

As a hospital carrier, the *Duke of Rothesay* also had her instructions for D-Day-plus-2 —to contact a guardship stationed off the Normandy coast and being thence directed to "Mulberry" where several of the crew were wounded by flying shell splinters, the result of very heavy aerial activity. For her first few days the *Rothesay* was engaged in collecting casualties from merchant and Navy vessels anchored offshore, but eventually a more direct contact was made with the land forces, notably at Juno beach-head and the synthetic port of Arromanches, when she took off wounded from the shore either in her own craft or from army "ducks."

Like the *Lancaster*, this vessel later saw service at the ports of Ostend, Dieppe and Cherbourg, and up to March 10th, 1945, had carried 23,960 Allied casualties, steamed 12,697 miles, and made 62 trips to either France or Belgium.

So this particular story of the L.M.S. Fleet could go on. The *Princess Maud* sailed from Weymouth Bay with an American task force the evening before D-Day, later being the first cross-channel troopship to enter Ostend. The *Princess Margaret* carried commandos, the S.S. *Dearne* stores and other cargoes. They, and others, did their job in full keeping with the highest traditions of the British Navy.

That, then, is some small account of D-Day as it affected the L.M.S. Together with the other main-line organizations it had fulfilled its biggest contract of all. The troops, their arms and equipment, had been got through to the ports, and, in so doing, the nation's 600,000 railwaymen and women were amongst the first to taste the fruits of victory as it applied to their own particular war jobs. After everything they had endured, those fruits were sweet indeed.

CHAPTER FOURTEEN

L.M.S. RAILWAYMEN AND RAILWAYWOMEN

IN one way or another the huge L.M.S. staff forms a representative cross-section of the population of the British Isles. An odd 250,000 strong, they are drawn from all walks of life.

Something of what they did during the war has been broadly recorded in the preceding chapters. Without them the Company would have stood still—no locomotives would have run, no ships' propellers would have revolved, nor would one single bolt or nut or cartridge case have been produced in the railway workshops.

Prior to 1939 it had taken years to build up that vast human machine, its directors, its executives, its office employees and all the many hundreds of different grades of manual and other workers. But that build-up had always been done with considerable care and selection—the physical and mental standards of juniors and of new employees being set high.

During peacetime, recruitment to the Company was always going on in a substantial way, and naturally enough the wastage due to resignations, retirements and deaths, was considerable. But when—during the war, there was added to that normal wastage a loss to the forces and elsewhere, of thousands of trained and experienced men, exceptionally difficult situations were created—for the loss coincided with a rapidly contracting labour market and a rapidly expanding volume of rail traffic.

From the early days of September, 1939, therefore, many of the L.M.S. staff were called upon to meet a complete change of duty, and nearly everyone undertook additional work out of all proportion to peacetime commitments. In the "shops," for instance, to obtain every ounce of production, the standard week, in the grim days of 1940, was raised to one of 66 hours, and it was not unusual for men to work up to 88 hours for long periods, this involving seven days a week without a break.

The same sort of conditions were going on elsewhere, many emergency sections being formed to operate "round the clock" hours, and many operatives, accustomed to day shifts, being called upon to work through the blackout of a wartime night. Upheavals and adjustments like this were extensive, not least in the domestic arrangements of an employee's own home.

Frequently, too, the new way of life entailed living away from home, and where shortage of accommodation was acute—as often happened—the Company did its best to alleviate the position by providing camping coaches and kitchen cars, together with recreation in the shape of games and wireless.

As the war developed the intensified industrial output and the influx of Allied troops made unprecedented demands on the organization as a whole, and to meet them necessitated the retention of men due for retirement, the bringing back of those who had already retired, and the employment of women. Indeed at the end of November, 1944, it was estimated that between 35 and 40 per cent. of the Operating Department's staff of 137,000 were employed in a temporary capacity. And remarkable it was how well everyone settled down to the new work with all the trials of the blackout and the blitz, and with particularly hard and long hours of work.

Recruitment and the training of staff was always a problem. In normal times the newly joined employee had ample opportunities to become acquainted with his job, spending a period in the lower or starting grades alongside an experienced hand. But under war conditions it soon became clear that there would not be enough suitable men coming along from the starting grades to fill vacancies in the higher. As the months wore on, therefore, only one substantial source of labour was still available—the country's womenfolk—and in due course they were engaged for those beginners' jobs in a really big way, steps being taken to give them every encouragement and assistance to learn the ropes.

But still the demands for qualified man-power were unsatisfied, and with the recruitment of men eventually dropping to small proportions—so again, there was only one solution—that these same women take on ever more and more important jobs. Gradually, then, this too was done until finally they came to be employed in such key posts as passenger guards and signalmen, thus releasing men working in these grades for similar, but more important duties elsewhere.

Training women for employment as ticket collectors, porters, vanmen and so on is not difficult, but it is a very different proposition when it comes to guards and signalmen. Nevertheless, training and tuition were started on specially selected candidates, and so successful did the venture prove, that by the end of 1944 there were on duty with the Company no less than 377 women guards and 623 signalwomen.

It was the same in many other railway departments, and it was this large scale employment of women which unquestionably helped to relieve a very difficult situation. Indeed, they finally worked in nearly 250 different railway grades, including such diverse jobs as concrete workers, sailmakers, assistant architects, fitters, electricians, boiler cleaners, weighbridge men, painters, lock-keepers, stablemen and even blacksmiths! At one time the total number employed by the Company amounted to 39,000, some 17 per cent of the whole staff.

It was all a very remarkable achievement and perhaps one of the happiest features of the new set-up was the readiness with which the regular staff adopted the newcomers, cheerfully helping them over their initial hurdles and displaying a fatherly care in their development. Without such human interest so freely given, the task of training entirely inexperienced individuals—and this applies to men as well as women—would have been impracticable.

Outside their regular jobs the staff undertook many other duties; the Home Guard, for example—whose fine record is characteristic of much that was done elsewhere. The appeal by the Prime Minister—the Rt. Hon. Winston Churchill—in the early summer of 1940, "to fight on the beaches, on the landing-grounds, in the fields, in the streets and in the hills," might well have included the railways, for the railwaymen's response was immediate and exceeded all expectations.

At that time the L.M.S. was being tried as never before, in coping with the immense difficulties of evacuating the B.E.F. from Dunkirk. Nevertheless, 46,000 of the Company's staff offered themselves for service and were enrolled.

The country was in a fix and the railwayman knew it. No one was better acquainted with the general layout of the permanent way and railway structures than he was, and no one could better appreciate the havoc which sabotage might inflict on bridges, telephone exchanges, tunnels and signal cabins.

Almost overnight, therefore, this large force had been well posted over the vast system, there being few really vulnerable points that had not their guard of alert men—little armed, it is true—but ready to resist to the limit of their powers.

Although the Home Guard was fated never to be tested in battle, seldom—outside the field of actual fighting—has human endurance been more tried. Working long railway hours, far beyond normal, they yet found time, in addition to doing regular spells as guards and sentries, to turn up for parades and to perfect their knowledge in the use of weapons, street fighting and a hundred and one other martial duties.

As time wore on many railwaymen in the Home Guard helped during air raids and later, as the danger of invasion receded, in anti-aircraft duties.

And this would seem a fitting place to refer to those members of the staff who actually left the Company to serve with His Majesty's Forces, or who gave full-time service in Civil Defence. The L.M.S. record is a particularly fine one, and would in point of fact require a large volume to do full justice to, for the number who actually served totalled 44,375. In the long years of 1939–45 L.M.S. men would have been found on nearly every battlefield, and the Company is particularly proud of their achievements. Many army units were almost exclusively manned by trained personnel drawn from the railways—particularly the docks groups, movement control units, and the railway construction companies of the Royal Engineers.

Space does not allow a detailed account of their doings, but they held commissions in the Navy, the Royal Marines, the Army, the R.A.F., the A.T.S., the W.R.N.S., and the W.A.A.F., a clerk rising to the rank of lieutenant-commander, an apprentice to wing-commander, and a draughtsman to lieutenant-colonel. In the course of their service they received over 150 decorations and on 88 occasions were mentioned in despatches. One received the D.S.O. and Bar, D.F.C. and Bar, and twice medals awarded in the 1914–18 war were rewarded in this—a D.C.M. and an M.M.

It is sad to relate that over 1,500 of these gallant men laid down their lives in the service of their country, over 1,000 more being taken prisoner.

The mention of awards made to L.M.S. members of the services calls to mind the fact that many other decorations were given by H.M. the King to railwaymen actually on duty with the Company—some in the face of enemy action, others not. Of the former, 54 awards were made, the majority being granted for great gallantry during the blitz, and one of many such episodes has already been recounted in Chapter Nine.

Of the latter, an award to John Quinn of Coatbridge, a ganger of 45 with 22 years' service, may be recalled. Briefly, this is what happened:

A permanent way gang employed on the up main line at Whifflet, having been warned by the look-out man that a train was approaching, all stood clear. One of the labourers, however, a woman, moved back too far and on to an adjacent loop line where a pilot train was propelling some empty wagons. Knocked down and sustaining severe injuries to her feet, she immediately endeavoured to crawl out from behind the moving train, and hearing her screams, it was thus that her ganger, John Quinn, first saw her. What happened next is still not very clear, but in some miraculous way he was able to dive between two of the moving wagons, drop on to the track and thus crawl back below the advancing trucks until he reached her, and could hold her down until the train was brought to a standstill.

Although both the unfortunate woman's feet were subsequently amputated, Quinn's action undoubtedly saved her from further mutilation and probably saved her life. To railwaymen in particular, and they are those who can best judge the hazardous nature of that daring and gallant deed, this will long be remembered as an action of outstanding bravery.

Another extra job undertaken by the L.M.S. staff was salvage, and this eventually became one of the accepted voluntary tasks of nearly everyone—in fact, in course of time it was more of a habit. Something has already been said of paper and other salvage, but all sorts of queer fish came into the net—aluminium from a 1916 Zeppelin, a ton of wool gleaned from sheep fences, and a key bearing a label "The house belonging to this has been bombed, please accept for salvage."

Up and down the Company's system, station vied with station to swell the collections, even the canals adjoining the line being successfully fished with a shunting hook, while a passenger porter at Wigan, working solely in his spare time, contributed over 200 tons of different materials. Snow or rain, blitz or no blitz, salvage kept pouring in.

Thus the record of these additional activities of the staff might go on and on. There were fire fighting and rescue services, there were the W.V.S. and the well-known railway ambulance organization, and there was the work done by the 8,500 members of the L.M.S. Horticultural Society on lineside allotments, with which may be coupled the considerable efforts of the Fur and Feather Society, both making worthy additions to the nation's food supply, the former with vegetables, the latter by rabbit breeding and chicken rearing.

Nor must the Company's contributions to the War Savings Movement be forgotten, there being over 1,000 groups, and as an example of what was done the workshops alone invested £489,389. Apart from this, £171,000 was raised for the Red Cross Penny-a-Week Fund, and over 120,000 members helped finance the Comforts Fund for L.M.S. Prisoners of War—the final sum subscribed being £55,000.

Chief of Staff at the beginning of the war was Lord Stamp—Chairman and President—and any record of the L.M.S. in war or peace would not be complete without a tribute to this remarkable man. Economic Adviser to the Government and Director of the Bank of England, his death, through enemy action in April, 1941, was a severe loss, not only to the railway company but to the country as a whole.

Soon after the 1914–18 war, the late Earl Lloyd George described Lord Stamp as the greatest living economist, and it was as such and as an administrator that he brought the Company so successfully through the difficult inter-war years following the amalgamation of the railways in 1923. With the unique and happy gift of being able to translate into simple everyday terms the most abstruse and technical subjects he found in the L.M.S. organization unlimited scope for his monumental ability. In the early months of the war, Lord Stamp travelled for many days and nights visiting distant parts of the system, personally examining the new problems that had to be tackled and encouraging and helping the staff to overcome them.

There were, however, many others whose individual war story, in part or whole, would be worth telling. Stories extending from those of the higher executives to the most junior grades of all. And variously courageous many of them would be—from intrepid bravery in the face of danger to indomitable tenacity, working unremittingly at an office desk for years on end. Sometimes it meant the permanent undermining of health—even the sacrifice of life itself.

To look at the L.M.S. staff as individuals is impracticable. The subject is too vast. Yet to the non-railwayman, privileged to peep behind the scenes at odd moments during

WOMEN CLEANING L.M.S. LOCOMOTIVES, CAMDEN SHED

the war, many little mental snapshots will remain of those he saw. A figure here, a figure there—of a woman labourer in the "shops" working a 4-ton drop hammer; of the genial stationmaster at Crewe, who on being questioned about his heavy war responsibilities, modestly remarked, "Well, I just tried to keep things going;" of the signalman who having had his cabin roof removed by a bomb only asked that it be replaced as soon as possible, otherwise he'd catch his death of cold!

Yet many others will be remembered too—the enquiry office attendant dealing with 489 calls in seven hours; the oldest employee, a claims clerk, close on 80 years of age; a signalwoman, now a grandmother, employed in the box where her husband started work over 30 years ago; she, and the ganger who stoutly maintained he'd been awarded his B.E.M. not for himself alone but "on behalf of my men and myself."

In point of fact, however, it is not as individuals that the L.M.S. staff would wish to be remembered. Rather is it as a team—a team gigantic in its conception and in its manifold interests, but for all that essentially single-minded in its purpose—to see that the "lines behind the lines" were loyally served as served they were.

That is the story of the L.M.S. at War!

CHAPTER FIFTEEN

THE FUTURE

THE past is always a guide to the future. Of the many expedients necessary during the war, some will no doubt be required during the period of transition to normal peace conditions; partly because of the continued requirements of the Government, and partly because the ravages of the war cannot be made good quickly.

Compared with the standard of maintenance immediately before hostilities, the renewals and repairs which have fallen behind in the six years since August, 1939, represent in terms of money some £30,000,000—and all quite apart from the cost of making good the abnormal wear and tear caused by exceptional war traffic and by the damage due to enemy aircraft, "doodlebugs" and the long-range rockets.

Setting to rights the huge L.M.S. house will necessarily be a lengthy process, for obviously it will take some time to bring back to their old jobs those of the key staff who were transferred to the outside factories in 1940, and those who joined up in the forces; nor must it be forgotten that timber, upholstery, tin, rubber and other materials will for a while be in short supply. It is likely, therefore—to take one specific case—that the building and renewal of passenger carriages (so seriously depleted during the war) will require several years before complete restoration is brought about, and in that time there is every likelihood that the passenger traffic will be particularly heavy. Replacement or reconditioning of the cross-channel steamers will also not be accomplished in a matter of months, and here again passengers will be most affected. It can, however, be anticipated that there will be a gradual but steady development of train and steamer services, not only in numbers and in speed, but in a general standard of comfort, particularly on long-distance journeys.

For locomotives and wagons, and for the permanent way itself, the arrears will be appreciably less than for carriages, but for station buildings very heavy outlay will be necessary; and, too, at a time when the demands for labour and material will be at their peak and when the country must give priority in rebuilding the tens of thousands of British homes destroyed by the enemy. The leeway here is big, especially so in decoration, due to the continuous and pressing demands, made even before hostilities started, for "gunnery over paintwork."

Indeed, it has been computed, that to pay for the effects of the war, to overtake the lag in new construction, and to meet the ordinary current requirements in the five years 1945–50 some £120,000,000 must be disbursed.

Such a huge sum will naturally give extensive and regular employment to many people, although that is not its primary purpose. For the aim will be to clear up the mess made by the war, to restore the old peacetime facilities of travel and to extend those same facilities even further, so that those who travel daily to and from their work, or those who make longer journeys for business or for pleasure, may do so in the greatest possible comfort.

We are facing in Britain a future of great change; immense problems require to be solved if liberty and common weal and efficient transport are to be served. All the skill and practical experience which this country can command will be needed. The record of the L.M.S. organisation and management in peace as well as in war is one which those who will have the task of carrying on the work might study with interest and advantage.

The future is to those who shape it, and the time for shaping is now. Already plans have been sanctioned, which, in their total, will cost over £140,000,000. In going ahead, so far as the limitations imposed by the labour and material shortages will allow, with schemes of modernization and improvement, the L.M.S. is giving practical evidence of its determination to improve upon the high standard of service which it was able to offer to the trading and travelling public before the war.

INDEX

H23 415 080 2

A CHARGE
IS MADE FOR
REMOVED OR
DAMAGED
LABELS.

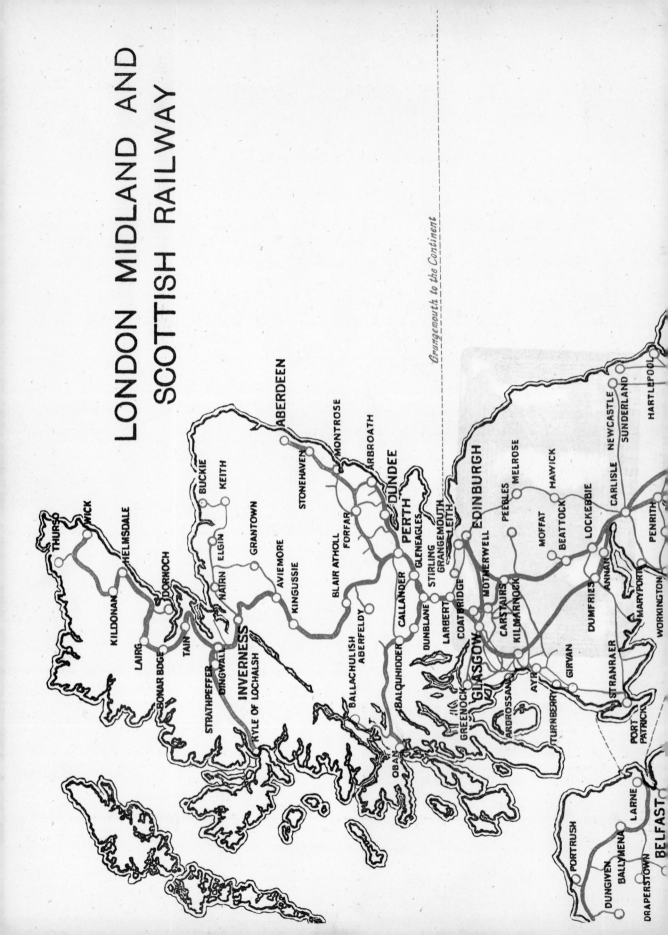